01P1

# CRITIC'S EYE

*Other books by Maurice Grosser*

PAINTINGS IN PUBLIC

THE PAINTER'S EYE

# CRITIC'S EYE

---

MAURICE GROSSER

THE **BOBBS-MERRILL** COMPANY, INC.
A SUBSIDIARY OF HOWARD W. SAMS & CO., INC.
*Publishers* • INDIANAPOLIS • NEW YORK

Acknowledgment is given to *The Nation* and to *National Review* to reprint material originally published by them.



PRINTED IN THE UNITED STATES OF AMERICA

*First Printing*

LIBRARY OF CONGRESS CATALOG CARD NUMBER: 62-12979

*For*

*ROBERT HATCH*

*GARRETT MATTINGLY*

*and*

*VIRGIL THOMSON*

*in gratitude*

*We'll go, brother Toby, said my father, whilst dinner is coddling, to the abbey of St. Germain, if only to see those bodies, of which Monsieur Sequier has given such a recommendation. I'll go see anybody, quoth my uncle Toby; for he was all compliance through every step of their journey. Defend me! said my father, they are all mummies. Then one need not shave, quoth my uncle Toby. Shave! No, cried my father, 'twill be more like relations to go with our beards on.*

LIFE AND OPINIONS OF
TRISTAM SHANDY, GENTLEMAN
BOOK VII, CHAPTER 27

# CONTENTS

# PORTRAITS OF PAINTERS

# *Bonnard, Chagall, Picasso*

THE PAINTING of our time comes in three distinct styles: fantasy, naturalism and abstraction, and three recent New York exhibitions—of Chagall, Bonnard and Picasso—present well-defined examples of each. Take Chagall to begin with. His field is fantasy. The subject of his pictures is the sentiment of love—the painter and his muse on a honeymoon, sometimes in a remembered Russian village, sometimes hovering in the air above nocturnal Paris. The muse offers the painter flowers as he stands before his easel. Half youth, half rooster, floating above the Seine and the Sainte Chapelle, he paints her picture. As a village accordionist in a farmyard, he plays for her: he is the cock, she the cow. They stand embracing in a mountain cottage. Angels in spring serenade her and bring her flowers.

There is no attempt at consistent sizes or perspective. We are in a dream world, where the size of things describes their relative importance, an interior world with no relation at all to that in which our bodies exist. The sentiment is charming. The paint surface has the richness and delicacy to be found only in the pictures of the School of Paris. One notices in the series of works here presented —they date 1910 to 1953—that as the painter matures, the color becomes progressively more decorative. It is built, for the most part, on a balance of red and blue, with bits of green, yellow, white, and brown for accent, not unlike the color pattern of French thirteenth-century stained glass. In one of these pictures, an early one, *La Femme aux Fleurs* of 1910, there is a trace of Cézanne's characteristic handling of paint—an influence which is usually to be found somewhere in the work of any painter of the school that flourished in Paris between the World Wars, and which, I believe, accounts for the great charm of surface that all these pictures possess. The pictures are all relatively simple, but skillful and quite honestly naïve—the most delightful of valentines. They are, of course, not the most serious paintings in the world, but they are saved from being mere decoration by the warmth of their sentiment.

Bonnard can scarcely be said to belong to the same epoch as Chagall and Picasso. Like Johann Sebastian Bach, he is a hangover from the past, a super-conservative. Just as Bach went on writing in the contrapuntal style while everyone else was playing with the *affetto* and with the intense expressiveness of accompanied melody, so Bonnard continued the Impressionists' preoccupation with the visual world long after everyone else had turned for subject matter to the evocation of historic styles, to the depiction of subjective states, or to the undermining of middle-class values.

Bonnard carried the representation of light by paint to a point of vibrancy the Impressionists themselves had not attained. His subject matter is that of the Impressionists: the charms and comforts of French domestic—food in the dining room, fruit and flowers from the garden, a child at his lessons, a landscape seen on an afternoon walk; all the pleasures of an ordered and peaceful existence.

These subjects, dangerous if not impossible for most painters of our time, Bonnard renders supremely well. There is no willful stylization whatsoever, though there is a great deal of omission. He omits, more often than not, all appearance of careful drawing, of school perspective, of any standard range of lights and shadows. There is a casualness about his painting, an ease that has nothing to do with the virtuoso, or even with professionalism. The effect is of something pleasantly and intelligently homemade.

The earliest picture shown in the exposition, *The Moulin Rouge* of 1896, has the brown shadow tones, the flattened perspective, and the slight effect of caricature of the early paintings of Vuillard. In the later pictures, caricature disappears and color effects take over.

The particularly fine *View of Vernon* of 1929—a landscape seen against the sun, an effect few painters have so well exploited—and the lovely *Still Life with Bottle of Red Wine* of 1942, with its white tablecloth and convincing false perspective, show how much this painter knew about the mutual alterations which take place when intense colors are put side by side—a subject no one understood as well as he. There is nothing capricious about these pictures. The painter is exploring with his eyes, and revealing on his canvas, the beauty of the world he sees around him. This is serious painting, at the same time unpretentious and complex, of a kind and quality not dissimilar to that of Renoir or Chardin.

The eleven Picassos exhibited range from 1932 to 1949, but the choice of pictures—all female heads or figures—give the exhibition unity. As usual in the work of this painter, the convention governing its execution is a reference to some earlier painting style. Here the stylistic evocation seems to be the Byzantine wall paintings of Catalonia.

In these eleven pictures, the thick boundary lines of the forms and the careful shaping of the empty spaces of background in between recall the frescos in early Catalan churches, while the hieratic immobility of the seated figures calls to mind the mosaics at Ravenna. There is no representation of a third dimension—not even by implication—nor any modeling in the figures. The composition is flat. The technique is that of the poster. The simplicity of the painted areas and the unvaried, brush-wide outlines render the pictures visible at any distance. They are designed to shout. When one remembers Picasso's long affiliation with the Surrealists, and their systematic program of subversion, one is led to suspect that the painter's intention is also to dismay.

The subject of these pictures, woman, is presented in her most unflattering aspects. Sometimes she is silly, as in the *Nu Couché* of 1932, where the romantic abandon of the body and the accompanying soft curves of the flowers and bed seem intended to parody Matisse. Sometimes she is wooden, as in the *Dame à la Fleur* of the same year, where the woman holding the flower seems herself a vegetable or flower form of insensitive shape and rowdy color. Or threatening, as in *La Dame à l'Artichant* of 1942—a woman enthroned, a head with bull's eyes and nostrils, legs crossed in irritation, and one hand holding a sceptre raised to command. Or watchful, as in the *Femme Assise* of 1946, a sort of African goddess, nude, hands on knees, mouth open, eye malignant. Or monstrous and comic, as in the *Femme Assise* of 1949, where the head and body melt into amoeba-like shapes and all the features have slipped out of place.

The usual explanation of pictures like these is that they are purely decorative, that their value lies in the simple beauty of shapes and colors which they undoubtedly possess. Of these particular canvases, however, this cannot be true. A decorative painting is a painting without urgent subject. Its shapes divert the eye but not the mind. A Mondrian, a Jackson Pollock, have no story. On the wall they become a neutral ornamentation in today's best decorative style and do not involve the spectator in any way.

But these Picassos are no more neutral than his famous *Guernica* which uses the identical technical devices to impress upon the spectator the painter's horror of war and Fascist cruelty. Here the same devices are employed, apparently, to satirize womankind. The means are powerful: Picasso is an old and supremely skillful workman. But the impatience, or flippancy, or whatever lies behind the painting of these pictures, divorced as it is from any moral framework, seems both loud and trivial—like an advertising slogan blared over a public address system.

What is really troublesome, however, about these pictures is not their sentiment. That is a question of personal taste. What is troublesome is a more serious, technical matter—the scale, which is to say, the amount of detail and elaboration allotted to the image depicted, compared to the picture's actual dimensions in feet and inches.

A large picture needs a great deal more detail than can be got by the mechanical enlargement of a small one. Unlike a photograph, a small picture blown up to big picture size invariably appears empty and thin. This is because, whether we know it or not, when we stand in front of a picture, our muscular sensations respond to the muscular tensions the painter felt when he put down the brush strokes. And we cannot help but compare the picture's size with the movements of the hand that made it. Thus, the size a picture happens to be is not a relative or accidental matter at all. It is an absolute quality measurable by the normal proportions of man himself. And the size of the brush strokes taken in relation to the picture as a whole—in other words, the scale—has as precise, and as powerful, emotional connotations as the key in which a piece of music is written.

In these, and in a great many similar pictures of Picasso's later years, the elaboration of detail bears no relation whatsoever to the size of the canvas. This is not true in his earlier pictures. Consider the wonderful carnival family in the Chester Dale Collection. There we have a large picture whose perfect scaling gives dignity to the figures and grandeur to the conception. But in these more recent pictures the scale is constantly faulty. They are small pictures mechanically blown up. As a consequence, they appear thin, overemphatic, and inhuman. They are too meager for the walls of a private house, where a painting must have a certain complexity if it is to withstand our constant inspection. They are even a shade too strident for the walls of a museum where comparison with the classical masterpieces could be disadvantageous.

It is perhaps fortunate for Picasso's reputation that his work is so largely known through reproductions, where the actual size of the original picture is not evident. But when one stands before the pictures themselves, the question arises of the painter's intention. If these are small pictures blown up to more impressive dimensions, then they are the work of a virtuoso seeking immediate effect. If this is the size of the pictures as originally conceived, then they are either the work of a hasty and brutal mind, or they represent the economies of a painter whose hand has lost its patience. One could wish in the work of so popular an artist more depth and less bravura.

Let us make no mistake: this is the work of a very great painter. The group is perhaps uneven in quality. One or two of the canvases are more interesting as jokes than as paintings. This is certainly true of one of the sculptures included—a nursing monkey whose face is formed by the body of a toy automobile. But even here the images are very difficult to forget. And leaving the three expositions, it is not Chagall and his charm one best remembers. It is Picasso who revolutionized every painting concept of his time; and Bonnard, also a very great painter, who changed nothing at all.

I have treated these expositions in some detail because the styles of these three painters define the three approaches to painting common in our time. Chagall's approach is that of all the other painters of fantasy—of Dali, Berman, Tchelitchew, of the Neo-Romantics and Surrealists, the group known as "Magic Realists," and the rest. These painters take for subject matter an interior state—perhaps a dream, or an attitude toward intimacy or love, a romantic evocation of the past, or a mystical apprehension of nature—and present it in an appropriate painting idiom. The idiom may be anything from the loose generalization of Bérard, to the tight brushwork of Cadmus, or Max Ernst's systematic use of accidental paint patterns. But with this variety of means and subject, all fantasy painting has this in common: its subject matter could conceivably have literary expression. It is poetic painting. Its popular and commercial aspects are stage design and advertising art.

Naturalism, the second approach, exemplified here by Bonnard, is as old as painting itself. It is the great tradition of painting. It is continued in our time by any number of painters, such as Leonid, Stuempfig, Carzou, and myself, to mention only a few. It is bound up with no particular means of painting and with no specialized subject matter. The painter is looking at the outside world through the distorting optical system of his eye and brain. The outside world is continuously in flux: the mind that seeks to record it is never twice the same. The interplay of these two fluid elements offers unlimited variety. Remembering the variety of the work executed under this canon in the past, one is tempted to believe that this is still the painter's most fecund working method. However, the commercial and popular aspects of this kind of painting are so mercilessly condemned by the critical world today that the very words "Naturalism" and "Realism" have become scarecrows to frighten children and students.

Picasso illustrates the third possibility, abstraction. In fact, he is credibly claimed to have invented it. Here, the real image—an apple, a harlequin, or a mother and child—is generalized, abstracted from its particular individuality as a unique object, and depicted in a simplified vocabulary derived from another, possibly historical, style of art. Thus, the subject matter of the painting becomes not the image presented, but an analysis of a style of painting or a mode of composition.

This has become the standard painting method of our time, the best taught and the most publicized. It has one serious weakness: it easily degenerates into decorative pattern. As Gertrude Stein once remarked, a completely abstract picture will be either decorative or pornographic. Even as early as 1925, Classical Cubism had become a popular style of household decoration. Picasso himself, aware of this danger, had long before adopted as an anti-decorative discipline a variety of emotional and even violent subjects; and in 1927 he publicly condemned the Constructivist sets of Gabo and Pevsner for Henri Sauguet's ballet *La Chatte* as *"Cubisme pour les Galeries Lafayette"*—Cubism for department stores. This still remains the pitfall for abstract painting today.

Thus, three different painting manners are available to the painter of our time. Which one of them he adopts depends uniquely on his subject matter. If his subject is a comment on art itself—if he is engaged in making an analysis of a historical style, or in reducing painting to one of its basic elements of color, texture, composition or brushwork for the sake of visceral emotions which these things used pure can be made to arouse—then he is an abstract painter, and will necessarily employ the techniques invented and sanctioned by modern art. If his subject is fantasy, the depiction of a dream world, or a poetic ecstasy, or a compulsive interior state—subjects which would be incomprehensible without clear statement—then he will be driven to present them in some traditional and easily understood technique, as do Dali and the English pre-Raphaelites before him, or as do Max Ernst and Magritte. He will expound his mysterious theme in a vocabulary of clearly painted symbols, and the rather old-fashioned techniques by which this clarity is obtained are the essential elements of the magic realist style. But if the painter's subject is the objective world and how it looks to him, his best tool will be one of the modern adaptations of Impressionism.

Impressionism today is not the same thing as the Impressionism practiced in the last century. The most striking difference is that Impressionism has now completely abandoned formal pointillism. This method of producing tones with little distinct dots of pure color juxtaposed on the canvas has proved to be more laborious than useful. Furthermore, pointillism, like blue shadows and lavender tonalities, has become disagreeably associated with that academy of Impressionism which fell so firmly into disrepute some thirty years ago. But apart from this, most of the characteristics of Classical Impressionism have been retained—dependence for subject matter on light and nature, love of clear color, a constant use of the soft and varied edge and of the brush stroke that breaks across the form—and that most important of all Impressionist contributions, the discipline of spontaneity by which each picture is painted as an improvisation.

So, as one can see, the way a painter chooses to paint is dictated entirely by his subject matter. The painter of fantasy tells a subjective or poetic story, using pictorial symbols and visual devices instead of words. The naturalistic painter tries to share with others the world he believes to lie in front of his own eyes. The subject matter of the abstract painter is art itself.

For the last thirty years we have tried to convince ourselves, to our great confusion, that the value of a work of art lies in the simple perfection of its shapes and colors—in what Clive Bell once called its "significant form." Now, in the middle of the century, it is about time to recognize that shapes and colors are only a means, and that the art of painting—like any other art—is a form of communication.

# *More Picasso*

SOME three hundred works by Pablo Picasso are being shown this summer at the Museum of Modern Art of New York in honor of the artist's seventy-fifth anniversary. Picasso is the most inventive painter of our time. What we call modern art is largely made up of the innovations he originated and exploited. The variety of his painting methods, the multiplicity of his styles, and the vivacity of his ideas have always dazzled. He is the one painter of our time with serious claim to genius. And now since more than fifty years have passed since his influence began to be felt, one should like to make some sort of definitive evaluation of his work and try to find its place in history.

As Gertrude Stein, one of Picasso's earliest admirers, pointed out, a contemporary work cannot fail to be interesting because it is about the things that are particularly interesting to us at that time. But it is not likely to strike us as beautiful. Instead, it will appear troublesome and ugly because the things that are the most interesting to us at a particular time are precisely the things we find most unfamiliar and disturbing. Consequently, it is always difficult to put any sort of final appraisal on a contemporary work. It is interesting or not, and that is all that can be said. If it is very good it will either be ignored—like Cézanne's work—or create a scandal—like Impressionism. It is only later, when times have changed and the subject of the work of art is no longer a disturbing or antagonizing part of our living, that the work can become beautiful. At that point we can detach ourselves from what the work was about and begin to see how well it was done.

Today the work of Picasso is no longer contemporary. Even the most recent paintings are in a familiar style; in the last twenty-five years there has been little radical change—except perhaps for an added brilliance—either in his technical approach or in his choice of image. And it has at length become possible to sort out the pictures according to quality and to understand more clearly the painter's intentions.

All this is made much easier by the excellent chronological arrangement of the exhibition here and relative completeness of the sampling. One notices in the earliest works the imitations and stylistic uncertainties always characteristic of the talented young. The faces—of *The Woman in Blue,* of the *Dwarf Dancer,* of the figures in *Le Moulin de la Galette*—have that flamboyant and eager toughness affected by Beardsley and the *fin-de-siècle* painters. Pictures are begun in one style and finished in another. Even in the *Woman Ironing,* as late as 1903, the mannered and sentimental treatment of the head is out of keeping with the quiet and accurate drawing of the arms and hands.

Then suddenly something happens, a flowering, a maturity. *The Boy with Pipe* and the *Boy Leading a Horse,* both of 1905—like the miraculous *Jugger's Family* in Washington—are images one cannot forget, painted in the most direct and unpretentious of painting styles. Uncertainty, brashness, even pathos are gone. The painter has disappeared, the work itself has come to life and speaks with a directness that only the greatest artists have ever managed to accomplish.

Picasso was then twenty-three. This particular sort of lyricism he never repeated. Probably he could not. His fantastic success had already begun. Perhaps that is why the pictures of the next few years seem unevenly painted. The portrait of Gertrude Stein and the *Woman Combing Her Hair* of 1906 again, as in the very early work, have heads in one style and hands and bodies in another. The *Two Nudes* of the same year (much less successful than the drawings for it) and *Les Demoiselles d'Avignon,* a fairly sketchy canvas where little but the heads have any sort of finished execution, both are more interesting as stylistic experiments than as completed pictures. It is not until one arrives at the Cubist period beginning in 1910 that Picasso seems again to be painting in a unified style. These subtle grays, the crisp brushwork, the balanced composition, and the tantalizing glimpses of the subject seen through a sort of prismatic dislocation render these pictures the perfect and perhaps the most provocative portion of his work. This was a manner that held his interest for more than ten years. But the elaborate game of textures which the early Cubism so quickly became—patterns of paper cutouts, of false wood, of confetti, with their wonderful wit and half-hidden references to the basic subjects of painting—shifted the painter's attention from the serious problems of painting in oil to the more superficial problems of pure decoration.

It was not until 1922, when he went to Rome with Diaghilev to design the sets and costumes for Eric Satie's ballet *Parade* and there discovered Graeco-Roman mural painting, that he again investigated the problems of painting in the round. The result was a series of heavily sculptural "Neo-Classical" figure compositions. The smaller among these pictures seem more successful than the large ones. These later, though monumental in conception, are a bit wooden and certainly over-pink. Few of these oils are as pleasing as his drawings of the period, some of which—*Diaghilev and Selisburg,* the *Two Peasants,* and *Dr. Claribel Cone*—with their wiry line, are among the most beautiful of his works. And the picture of his son Paul in harlequin costume, of 1924, done in oil but in the same linear style as the portrait drawings, is one of his most direct and touching pieces.

From this point the work becomes more brilliant, more violent, and less humanly interesting. The canvas is often larger than the subject deserves, and although the pictures are always pulled off in a masterly fashion, the painting itself is frequently either skimped or brutal. The joke of how the human figure can be recognized in spite of all distortions by the presence of teeth and breasts is endlessly repeated, frequently with wit but generally with hatred, achieving sometimes the savage disgust of the *Reclining Nude* of 1936—an amoebic form overlooked by moon and stars—or of the *Woman Dressing Her Hair* of 1940—a harpy all the more terrifying on account of the solidity of her projecting forms. The color is sometimes handsome, sometimes even quite astonishing, as in the *Girl Reading* of 1934, where the bright yellow of the lamp and the mauve, lilac, and white of the hands and face give the exact effect of artificial light, and there is a marvelous evocation of a child's drawing in *Night Fishing in Antibes* of 1939. But even before the *Guernica,* large scale and hard outline seem to have become a permanent part of the painting method, and many of the later pictures seem like posters intended chiefly to advertise the manufacturer's name.

Among the most recent pictures here, the most interesting are perhaps *The Portrait of a Painter, after El Greco* of 1950, mordant comment in brown and black on the sixteenth-century Spanish style, the *Winter Landscape* in dark greens of Vallauris of the same year, and the very engaging portrait of the infant *Paul in Polish Costume* of 1948. Otherwise there is little that is completely free of malice or bravura. The series of fifteen canvases painted during the winter of 1954, inspired by *The Women of Algiers* of Delacroix, arrives at nothing more impressive than a pastiche of Matisse.

A progress such as this, from the tenderest human sympathy to the bitterest misanthropy, from the most impersonal and delicate mastery of paint to bleak outline and hard embroideries, from the lyricism of personal sentiment to the public utterances of a loudspeaker, is unusual in a painter. Painters, in general, once mastery is acquired, do not degenerate unless there is present some vice of character or some unmanageable element in the career. Here I believe the trouble has been publicity.

Selling pictures by publicity is a special technique invented by our time. Under ordinary circumstances it is impossible to sell pictures by advertising methods. The normal picture-buying public is too disdainful of unauthorized opinion to be influenced by outside pressure, and too small to be touched by the large-scale methods devised to influence groups. Publicity's discovery in this field is that if the painter can be presented as a superhuman figure, a new and larger public can be reached, a public not necessarily interested in painting but very much interested in genius. What is being sold is not a painting but a painter's fame.

Picasso among the artists has been publicity's greatest success and, I believe, its greatest victim. Only the necessity to astonish which publicity imposes could have driven him into such courses of eclecticism, mystification and virtuosity. Certainly, a great deal of his work will remain as the finest of our century. But I suspect that he will be remembered less as the painter who liberated art from dead traditions than as the man who could not afford to respect any.

# *Gaudi and Mondrian*

THE WORK of the Catalan architect, Antoni Gaudi, so admired by Salvador Dali, is on display at the Museum of Modern Art. The material consists of photographs, plans, and reproductions of detail assembled from Barcelona by Professor Henry-Russell Hitchcock. At the same time the Solomon R. Guggenheim Museum is showing an extensive exhibit of Piet Mondrian's earlier canvases and drawings. One could not ask for a more interesting opposition. Gaudi was the most extreme—and indigestible—of the architects and designers who created the "Art Nouveau" style of the 1900's, while Mondrian achieved the perfect expression of the esthetic on which is based the architecture of our own time.

"Art Nouveau" (though Gaudi seems to have initiated it in Barcelona some ten years earlier) appeared first in Brussels and Paris in the 1890's. The French called it "le Style Metro" after the Paris subway entrances designed in the manner—bronze structures resembling rising and drooping flower stems. The style's distinguishing characteristic was its constant use of the weak curve—a curve which begins as if it were intending to spiral, and then, instead of coming to an end with a snap, as it does in the Gothic or Baroque, turns upon itself with an "S" motion and proceeds to go somewhere else. The style, nonetheless, can be considered an extension of the Gothic. It made use of naturalistic flower and vegetable forms of decorative motives as the Gothic did (although in Gothic the poppy, the iris, the cattail, and the waterlily are not to be found) and its immediate origin was the medievalism of the pre-Raphaelite painters. In the Gothic, however, architectural movements are vertical; if things do not move upward, at least they stay still.

Even in the work of the English medievalists of the nineteenth century—as can be seen in the ironwork of the old Hotel Chelsea which comes from the studio of William Morris—the naturalistic flower motives are usually held fast in a fixed, architectural grill. But in "Art Nouveau" the sinuosities of vegetable form are no longer contained in a geometrical matrix; they replace it. They become the architectural structure. The architect no longer denies the force of gravity; he illustrates it, and viscosity and fluid motion as well. The bronze violets of a candelabra rise, are pulled back to earth, and rise again. Water-lily stems on a vase drift in opposing currents. The substance composing the lettering of a sign slowly creeps downward like tar in the sun and thickens the characters' bases.

Gaudi did not confine himself to a vocabulary of flower forms. His greatest monument and perhaps the most astonishing ecclesiastical monument of our time, the Church of the Sagrada Familia, begun in 1885, would seem to contain almost every form in nature. The building was left unfinished at the architect's death. There exists only a transept, a triple-arched porch surmounted by four huge steeples whose shape, like elongated ears of corn, is reminiscent of Central Africa. The façade is in a sort of free Gothic. There are palm trees, turtles, and snails, flights of birds attached to the stone work by only the tip of a wing, dripping forms that might be moss or stalactites, trumpeting angels, interior columns swaying in slight spirals like the trunks of growing trees, no two alike. And high over the central portal an enormous octopus spells out with his tentacles the IHS of Christ—extraordinary, fascinating, and a little repellent in a way that seems both Coney Island and particularly Barcelonese.

The Casa Mila, an apartment house begun in 1905, is an equally astonishing work. This has none of the Sagrada Familia's symmetry. It resembles a sea cave hollowed out by the tides. The exterior pillars and balconies are of stone, pitted as if by wind and sand. The ceilings have ripple marks and linear mosaic patterns like light reflected up from the surface of water. The ironwork of the railings and balconies is kelp. The chimney pots are giant sea anemones or polyps and the roof top surges in ridges and troughs like waves at sea.

All of the work without exception is ingenious, rich, elaborate, skillfully designed, and carefully executed. Its "bad taste," its "Luna Park" aspect, only renders it more lively and entertaining. It is nevertheless more than a little oppressive. This, I think, is a question of weight.

Was Gaudi perhaps a fat man? I do not know. At any rate he must have had an exaggerated awareness of the pull of gravity. One realizes from the photographs of Santa Coloma de Cervello, with its leaning rough stone pillars, that he was a virtuoso in the calculation of mechanical strains. His columns turn and twist to follow torque and vector. His stonework sags to demonstrate its mass. His furniture bends in supporting its own weight, and mirrors and door-panels slip down in their frames. Everything is semi-fluid, like stiff molasses or warm chocolate creams. (Dali calls it edible architecture.) Everything is sinking upon our heads. It is precisely this—the tendency to fall, to subside, to melt—which makes "Art Nouveau" so difficult to revive as a decorative style in spite of the beauty of much of its furniture, and which places the work of Gaudi, despite his undeniable genius, outside the useful traditions of architecture.

The Mondrians on display at the Guggenheim Museum date from 1904 to 1943, with emphasis on the pictures of earlier years. Up to 1910 the work is that of a well-trained draftsman and a remarkable colorist, master of every color style from close harmonies in subdued tones to the most brilliant Fauvist orchestrations. The subjects—a tree, a dune, a windmill—are rather excuses for color than significant in themselves. But the color harmonies could not be more beautiful.

In 1911 the painter left Holland for Paris and Cubism. He simplified his color to the gray-blue, dun, and black which one knows so well in the Cubist work of the period, and schematized his drawing to an exceptionally simple Cubist pattern. The subjects are principally trees and are quite recognizable. The line has been reduced to short vertical and horizontal strokes and to sections of simple curves. Somewhere around 1914, as can be seen in a picture entitled *Façade,* Mondrian abandons all Naturalistic evocation, the curved lines disappear, and one begins to find the strict canons of abstraction we ordinarily associate with this painter's work.

These canons, however, are not yet complete. Just as in his Cubist pictures, where the tree forms in the center of the canvas do not extend into the corners, the composition of these early Abstractions is concentrated in the center. In *Façade,* in the drawings *Cathedral* and *Pier and Ocean,* in *Composition with Lines (Plus-Minus)*—all from 1914–17 and executed in close patterns of horizontal and vertical dashes—the lines and crosses falling in the corners are either painted in paler tones or eliminated altogether. In abstract painting of this sort, something like this is necessary. Otherwise these rectangular marks, underlined and accented by their nearness to the rectangular corners of the frame, would upset the balance of the composition and lead the eye out of the picture. This is in fact, precisely what does happen in two later works of 1919 done in regular checks *(Composition. Checkerboard, Light Colors* and *Composition. Checkerboard, Dark Colors)* which on account of their even pattern and insistent corners resemble nothing so much as sections of a bathroom floor. The early Cubists frequently avoided this difficulty by painting in an oval. Mondrian learned to avoid it by working on a diamond-shaped canvas and thus eliminating the troublesome horizontal corners altogether. He finally solved the problem by abandoning his regular, all-over pattern for an open and unsymmetrical plaid.

Plaids such as these, I am given to understand, were once commonly used in art schools to analyze students' compositions. The important objects in a picture were enclosed in bands parallel to the sides of the canvas, whereupon the rightness of the space divisions in the picture itself could be judged by the intrinsic interest of the resulting plaid. Here, however, the plaid is the thing sought for. Contrary to what one might think, it is not easy to do. Holding the eye with such paucity of means—no lines but the vertical and horizontal, two or three simple colors, no gradation of tone, no visible brush stroke, and all done in a careful freehand imitation of mechanical exactitude—demands the most accurate feeling for space division and the most painstaking effort. Nor are these pictures easy to imitate. One has only to see them beside others of the school (as one can see in the Gallatin collection in the Philadelphia Museum) to be aware of their superiority.

Unfortunately, these later pictures are not holding up. The earlier ones, painted with more spontaneous brushwork on a rougher canvas, are still handsome, clean, and well preserved. The later ones, executed in smooth paint on a smooth canvas prepared with heavy priming, already show the irreparable cracks which such a ground will suffer from even the slightest blow. And their pure and even whites accept the patina of age no more gracefully than do the flat façades of our modern buildings. It seems a pity that these pictures were not executed in some more resistant material.

Perhaps they were. These orderly grids with their carefully adjusted proportions have been of enormous use to typography and to architecture. This contribution may turn out to be Mondrian's most enduring monument. He is the one celebrated painter of our time whose individual pictures are difficult to remember. One remembers the general pattern more vividly than one can recall a particular work. But it is also due to the perfection of these pictures' proportions that the world of our time is so unforgettably stamped with Mondrian's memory.

# *Courbet*

THE LARGEST and finest exhibition of Gustave Courbet ever got together in this country is on view at the Philadelphia Museum of Art. The eighty-six pictures, assembled from museums and collections here and in Europe—four even from the Louvre—illustrate the entire range of the painter's work, from the student compositions and self-portraits of his youth to the Swiss landscapes of his last years.

Courbet's life was long and turbulent. Son of a wealthy farmer from a village near Besançon, handsome and talented, he arrived in Paris in 1840, at the age of twenty-one. One imagines him as a restless and energetic man, intensely ambitious, loudly convinced of his abilities, an intolerant Republican. At first accepted by the Salon, and then bitterly opposed on account of his insistent realism, he eventually overcame all opposition and was acknowledged even by his enemies as a genius. In 1871, having joined the Commune, he was pronounced responsible, as its most prominent and politically active painter member, for the destruction of Napoleon's column in the Place Vendôme, and was sentenced to six months in jail. After his release, his case being reopened, he fled to Switzerland, where he died at the age of seventy-eight, his goods and pictures confiscated. His place in the history of French painting is that of being the first of the Realists and thus precursor of Impressionism.

This celebrated Realism does not appear in the early self-portraits on view. These are rather in the high Romantic tradition: the painter picturing himself as a beautiful and disdainful young man, seated on a hillside with pipe, book, cane, and dog, glaring up at the spectator as if annoyed at the interruption of his meditation; as a guitar player in beard and Giorgione clothes; and as a Florentine sculptor, mallet and chisel in hand, poetically relaxed in the midst of nature. The Romantic phase was quickly over. With his stubborn Republicanism and his farm background, he soon evolved a style of painting which, in contradistinction to the Liberal Romanticism of Delacroix and to the Tory Classicism of Ingres, became known as Realism. That is to say, he abandoned the Romantic subject matter of the exotic, the tragic, and the marvelous (such as Delacroix's *Massacre of Chios* or his *Death of Sardanapalus*), and took instead as subjects for his pictures the commonplaces of life around him (such as his *Burial at Ornans,* his native village, or his famous *Bonjour, Monsieur Courbet* in which the painter depicts himself being saluted on a country road by his richest collector—a picture also entitled, less modestly, *Fortune Greeting Genius*).

Besides giving up Romantic subject matter, Courbet cut himself free from all dependence on the Italian Renaissance and, in opposition to the smooth elegance of Ingres, adopted a downright and much more brutal way of painting. His chief technical innovation was a systematic use of the palette knife, by which he could obtain, with one tone pulled over another, the exact appearance of the textures of nature. The rocks, bark, foam, and foliage of his landscapes could not be more convincing. The other novelties of his work, and perhaps the most striking, were his ability to paint landscape without any poetic overtones, and the hitherto undescribed—and rather heavy—style of female beauty he celebrated.

This style of beauty one finds supremely well expressed in his *Spanish Lady* with her unbound hair and querulous mouth; and in the *Polish Exile* with her aristocratic reserve, her quiet hands and unquiet eyes—so much like Eakins in their psychological projection, but so much better. The two portraits of the Nodler brothers are even more powerful and disquieting as psychological studies, while the standing figure of Max Buchon, with hat in hand, cane, and almost ballet-dancer stance, is certainly the inspiration for the similar portraits by Manet. This is all very fine painting. Many of the open landscapes, always empty and curiously lonely, are as convincing as Corot's. The color, however, is seldom as exact. Courbet's eye for color tones is not as nice; and since he almost always employs the academic formula of cool lights and warm darks, most of the pictures, even those portraying the out-of-doors, have the brown shadows of objects painted under studio conditions.

The most curious aspect of Courbet's work, as it is presented here, is its unevenness. It seems impossible that the same painter could have painted both so well and so badly. Perhaps painting, as he frequently did, large pictures for large public exhibitions, he often worked beyond his fatigue level. The clearest suggestion of this is in the *Demoiselles du Village,* shown here in two versions. The subject is a green and rocky meadow in which three town-dressed ladies are conversing with a peasant girl. The smaller picture—called a sketch, though it is in every way complete—could not be finer. The larger version, blown up to standard Salon size of about six feet by ten, is cruder in color, laborious in drawing, spotty in composition, and the exquisite scaling of the figures to the landscape is no longer there.

Others of the larger pictures with Salon subjects in Salon sizes are even less successful. But size does not always seem to be the chief difficulty. Many smaller pictures are just as unfortunate. The Lesbian *Awakening,* in which a brunette nude drops rose petals on the eyelids of a sleeping blonde, is harsh in color and insensitive in drawing. *A Reclining Nude* of 1858 looks like a particularly poor example of Eilshemius. And two minor forest pictures of stags in snow seem like woolly "buckeyes" done for the calendar trade. Whereas the large *Deer in Covert,* from the Louvre, and the wonderful *Quarry,* from Boston, with huntsmen, horn, dogs, and Courbet himself as central figure, are two of the finest forest pictures ever painted.

Several of the weak pictures here shown are perhaps not wholly Courbet's work. In *Dressing the Bride,* for instance, a large interior with some fourteen figures, the disparity between the well-planned composition and the incompetence of its execution suggest a beginning by Courbet, carried further by another hand. Similarly, the *Hunt Picnic* with its amateurish painting and incongruous scale must be either a pastiche or a remarkably unsuccessful restoration. And is it possible that the portrait of Courbet in prison could be by Courbet himself? It first appeared publicly in 1903 when presented by Courbet's sister Jacqueline to the town of Ornans. It is not signed. Perhaps the old lady was remembering badly. It is so uncouth in drawing, color, and composition that it seems more likely something done by a visitor or student, a lesson given by the painter to while away the tedium of jail.

In an adjoining room are some of the Philadelphia Museum's latest acquisitions—two Delacroix studies, a figure piece by Corot, a still life of a hare by Chardin and a small oil by Daumier. Comparison with these is not to Courbet's advantage. The Delacroix are more sure in their drawing; the Corot and Daumier have livelier color; even the fur in Chardin is better painted. Not that Courbet lacks skill or talent or invention. He had more than almost anybody. But he seems never to have matured as a painter, never to have gained complete control of his talent. The trouble most probably lay in his taste for celebrity, and in his addiction to party politics. With both a professional and a political revolution to occupy his energies, with so many "great" pictures to execute and so many eager disciples to distract him, how could he always find time for the finer points of his trade? He remains, for all his genius and for all his mental activity, the most uneven workman in the history of French art.

And yet, despite all this, Courbet is a precursor and a Modern.

Daumier, Delacroix and even Corot, however sympathetic we may find their work, line up with the Old Masters, whereas Courbet is unmistakably on our side of the fence. The palette-knife technique of his forest interiors directed the Impressionists to their theories of broken color and unified surface tension. And his particular version of Realism led straight to their doctrine of the innocent eye and its unprejudiced view of nature. These are still the basic principles of our painting today.

# *Monet*

MORE than a hundred landscapes of Claude Monet are on view at the Museum of Modern Art. The paintings range from a *Beach at Sainte-Adresse,* done in 1865, when the artist was twenty-five, down to the waterlilies and flower improvisations left unsigned in the studio at his death in 1926.

Monet was a prodigious worker. He must have turned out in his life some two to three thousand canvases. Any collection now got together, however large, can present only a sampling of this monumental production. The present show somewhat neglects the earlier pictures done under the influence of Boudin, with their gentle contrasts of warms and cools (though there is a wonderful *Gare Saint Lazare* with sooty locomotives steaming under the station's shed-like roof, all in grays and blacks). Emphasis is rather placed on the more characteristic and brighter-colored works of the middle and later years. Particularly memorable are a dark *Waterloo Bridge,* heavy with the traffic of a foggy evening; *Mount Kolsaas* in Norway, half visible through the mist; the *Palazzo da Mula* in Venice, in a dark blue dusk, and the *Palazzo Contarini* on a dark winter afternoon; and perhaps most splendid of all, the Metropolitan's *Rouen Cathedral* in the searing, blinding white of high noon.

There have been large Monet shows before but this apparently is the first to reassemble the scattered members of Monet's famous "series" since they were first exhibited. Here shown together are nine pictures from the *Haystack* series, seven from the series of *Poplars on the River Epte,* six of *Rouen Cathedral* and six of the *Japanese Footbridge* which spanned the lily pond in his garden in Giverny. These series one has always heard about but never seen—how Monet, to capture particular effects of light, would paint the same subject, day after day, for two or three years on end, using a series of canvases, and working on each of them as long as each particular effect would last—until, for example, the morning mist had lifted, or the rising sun had touched a certain leaf. This, after the age of fifty, became Monet's standard practice. There were fifteen of the *Haystacks* in his exposition of 1891. The *Poplars on the Epte* he did in so many versions that he was eventually forced to buy the trees themselves to prevent their being cut down in the middle of his painting them. And there exist some thirty *Rouen Cathedrals,* all different but all painted from the same second-story window.

To make possible such complex procedure, Monet adopted a radical simplification of the problems of composition. He ceased to compose in the classical sense. He did not arrange. Instead, like a photographer concentrating the emphasis of a print, he cropped. In all probability he used a small rectangular frame of the same proportions as his canvas—like the finder of a camera—to view his subject and determine just where the edges of his canvas would fall.

The Impressionist system of color he employed is fairly common knowledge—how colors could be mixed, not as pigments blended on the palette, but as spots of colored light blending in the beholder's eye. The extension of the system employed by Monet in the later pictures is less generally known. In this development, the landscape to be painted was thought of as if lighted on a stage—with the sun as a yellow spotlight, the sky as a bank of blue floods. Objects in shadow from the sun, but lit by the blue light of the sky, are colored blue by it. Things in shadow from both sun and sky are lit by the footlights made by sunlight on the ground, footlights which are red or orange if the ground is earth or clay, and green if there is grass. Distance is handled by treating the air itself as a tangible entity, and adding to the color of the distant objects the color of the intervening air—even on the clearest day never completely transparent. Furthermore, to compensate for the relative dullness of the indoor light by which the finished picture will be viewed, every tone put down is arbitrarily raised to the highest point of color saturation. Its chroma—that is to say its position on the color circle, its identity as a green-blue or orange-red—is preserved. But it is painted without any dulling, in paint as bright as possible. Thus a tan—which is considered as a dulled yellow—is transcribed as a bright golden yellow, a brown as a burnt orange, and a gray as a blue-violet or a bright pale blue.

All this together made up a system of painting that could be done by observation alone. It freed the painter from endless dilemmas of judgment and indecisions about taste. It rendered possible all sorts of hitherto impossible subject matters. And on account of the simplicities it provided, it was in large part responsible for the enormous productivity Monet was able to maintain in his later years.

This system is also what made the work at the same time so good and so uneven. The technical side of the pictures is always extraordinary—rich and supple and varied. Cézanne is reported as saying that Monet "was the most prodigious eye since there have been painters." But the taste and subject are sometimes considerably less satisfactory. A garish sunset in Venice is a garish sunset still. And the series of *Haystacks,* with all their exactitude of light and air and time of day, are dull in composition and trivial as pictures, simply because of their arbitrary triviality of subject matter. Monet himself must have realized the danger of such excessive simplification of motif, for in the subsequent series such as the *Poplars,* the *Cathedrals,* and the *Waterlilies,* the subjects used are more intricate and much more presentable.

The pictures in the exhibition done during the last years of the artist's life are on the whole inferior. Those of the *Japanese Foot-*

*bridge* series, painted when he was almost blind from double cataract, are harsh and gaudy in color, and quite disquieting in their melting, dripping forms. After an eye operation, his color vision rectified itself, and the pictures regain their serene and opulent tones. But though some of them are quite as interesting in their large and virtuoso manner as the earlier work, most of them seem to me singularly thin and empty—the work of a very old man. I suspect that they are admired because their principal merit is that their elaborate surface and thinness of image seem to prefigure one of the most formless modes of present-day Abstraction.

Be this as it may, a great painter has a perfect right not to please us if he wishes. And Monet, who remade all painting, who exercised even more influence on his contemporaries than Cézanne has exercised on the painters of our time, whose very style has become synonymous with Impressionism, was a very great painter indeed.

# *Seurat*

THE GREAT exhibition of the works of George-Pierre Seurat, got together by the Art Institute of Chicago, is on display at the Museum of Modern Art. The pictures are beautifully hung and lighted. There are some one hundred and fifty works, including four of seven large figure pieces—*La Grande Jatte,* a version of the *Three Models, Le Chahut* and *Le Cirque,* as well as the sketches and preparatory paintings for them—figure pieces, landscapes and almost a hundred drawings. Seurat's life was short. The pictures here represent the major portion of his work.

Seurat, as a very young man, had studied in the École des Beaux Arts. By 1880, at the age of twenty-one, he was already a proficient painter in the then new Impressionist style. The works of this time are small, painted with crosshatchings and spottings of bright pigments, the forms rounded and luminous, without outline or detail, the color glowing and strikingly successful in the rendition of sunlight and haze. It is at this point, also, that his characteristic style of black-and-white drawing first appears—a style in which there are no lines and no details, but only rounded masses in a fog of light and shadow. The edges of the forms are fuzzed to such an extent that one wonders whether Seurat were not myopic.

Shortly thereafter he began the studies for his first large pictures, *The Bathers* and *La Grande Jatte*. These preparatory sketches, particularly those for *La Jatte,* are some of the painter's most interesting work. In these Sunday strollers on the banks of the Seine he had found what all painters most desire, a large, absorbing subject. For two years he worked at it steadily, making twenty or thirty sketches, both of the unpeopled landscape background, and of the people who were to be in it. These he combined into a spectacular final study, the *Definitive Study for La Grande Jatte,* here on loan from the Metropolitan.

The color in the *Definitive Study* is wonderful. The brilliant sunlight and cool summer shadows are so pleasant and the recessive depth so convincing that one forgives the somewhat wooden and immobile figures. Something of the vivacity of the original sketches has been lost but the drawing still remains easy, the forms generalized but solid.

The finished picture is also handsome but much stiffer than the study. It is enormous—seven feet by ten. Renoir is said to have detested it. Most probably he found in its stiff figures a malicious parody of his own work. Certainly the color is flatter than in the study and the light less convincing. The figures are given hard, definite edges, like cut-out and colored cardboard silhouettes set up at varying distances in a perspective box. Most curious of all, on top of these silhouettes is superimposed a lacework of sharp detail of feature and costumes, nowhere prefigured in the studies—an artificial and irrelevant embroidery. It is as if Seurat were putting down by rote details he knew were there but had not actually observed—like a naïve painter who is forced to invent and remember since he has not been trained to see.

The subsequent work carries this naïve and detailed stylization even farther and with less success. The *Three Models* and the sketches for it are tight and labored, the drawing of the figures is inconsistent and weak. As for *La Poudreuse, Le Chahut* and *Le Cirque,* one has only to compare them with similar works by Degas and Toulouse-Lautrec to see how inferior they are in every respect. Their compositions are arbitrary and laborious, their drawing contrived and flat, their sentiment childish and, most surprising of all, they have no color. Seurat's vaunted color theories notwithstanding, they appear today a pallid mosaic of vaguely tinted dots. Their powdery tone, their stylized drawing and rigid, obvious composition, charming enough on a candy box or amusing perhaps in naïve work, are unacceptable from a major painter.

What could have changed this charming, sensitive, and minor Impressionist master into the contriver of such imposing and unwieldy images? Perhaps he was misled by theory. Seurat was a solitary, reticent man and a strict logician. Under the influence of Charles Henry, a writer on esthetics, he had come to adopt a set of absurd rules supposed to explain the effect of abstract pictorial elements on the emotions. Thus, gaiety was to be obtained by warm, light colors and ascending lines; calm, by a balance of warm and cold, and light and dark, and by the use of horizontals; sadness, by cold, dark colors and lines leading down. Rules such as these are nothing but inconsequent verbal associations and have nothing whatever to do with the art of painting. But Seurat, we are told, took them quite seriously. A further difficulty lay perhaps in Seurat's actual vision. To judge from the drawings and early paintings with their constant omission of detail, Seurat did not see in linear terms at all. If, as one imagines, his eyes did not focus normally, the sort of linear composition these rules demanded was an impossible and unnatural effort for him. As for his mathematically conceived color theories, if one is to judge from the last three works, either the theories were completely unfounded, or the works were executed in the most unstable pigments. *Le Cirque* I seem to remember from some twenty years ago as bright with mauve and purple. Perhaps the pictures have simply faded. But this is difficult to believe in view of the marvelous color the earlier work displays. And I am driven to conclude that for a painter, an *a priori* esthetic theory is a very dangerous business.

Though, in this case, not an unprofitable one. Seurat's high position in the world of art today is principally due, I believe, to the effect of these very theories. He was the first of the Impressionist-trained painters to turn for subject matter away from nature, and take as subject for his pictures the Impressionist method itself. And as the first of the modern Mannerists, it is he, rather than Cézanne, who is the progenitor of Modern art, itself a school of Mannerism.

Be that as it may, Seurat was a man of immense talent and energy, and the manner of these last pictures was probably only a passing phase. It is a great pity he died so young. At thirty-one a painter's life is just beginning. Think how little Cézanne had accomplished by then.

# *Renoir and Guttuso*

A LOAN exhibition of the works of Pierre-Auguste Renoir is being shown at Wildenstein's. The seventy paintings and eight or ten pieces of sculpture present the whole range of Renoir's work, from the precise drawing and grayed tones of the *Pont des Arts,* painted in 1868 at the age of twenty-seven, to the voluptuous forms and prismatic color of *The Concert,* done in 1919, the year of the painter's death. One regrets the absence of the celebrated pictures from the Phillips Gallery and from Boston of boating life on the Marne. But there is the *Moulin de la Galette* and the *Waitress from Duval's* to replace them.

What an easygoing man Renoir must have been! One understands his distrust for Seurat's intellectualized painting theories. Renoir did not work by theory; he depended on spontaneity and sensibility. Since he was a man of simple tastes—a sort of Saint Francis of the brush—he could allow himself the luxury of painting as he liked. And he liked the most pleasant things—pretty girls, presentable ladies and gentlemen, children with big eyes and clear complexions, fruit, flowers, and sunny landscapes—all the elements of a good world which his innocent, sensual eye transformed into a Third Republic Garden of Eden.

Since he did not work by voluntary formula, his painting style has great variety. Sometimes the paint is put down in tiny touches, thin and liquid; sometimes it is loaded. Sometimes the edges are neat; sometimes everything melts in a mist. A number of the pictures are in the Pointillist manner. There is even one done at L'Estaque of olives and pines and white, rocky hills which could be mistaken for a Cézanne, whom Renoir was then visiting.

Of all the Impressionists, Renoir has probably suffered most from time and restoration. And however little the pictures here may be tarnished, one still would like to have seen them as they came from the painter's brush. For color was Renoir's gift and passion. It is really only in his color that he conforms to the Impressionist idea. As Proust pointed out, he was, in sentiment, a belated Fragonard. Vlaminck has a pretty story about his color sense, of how Renoir, taking a walk with some other painters, left his overcoat behind in a field. They all returned to look for it. "There it is," said Renoir, pointing in the distance. "You can't tell what it is," said somebody, "it's too far away." "Oh, yes, I can," said Renoir. "It's black. There are no blacks in nature."

At the same time as this, a large and handsome show of the Sicilian painter, Renato Guttuso, is being held at the ACA Gallery. Guttuso is one of the most brilliant of the contemporary Italians, a vigorous draftsman, a lively colorist, and a master of differentiated paint textures. His subjects are not unlike those of the contemporary Italian cinema—ordinary people and things. Whatever he paints is seen from an unexpected point of view—people crossing a street, each one different, each one in a hurry; a farm hand eating spaghetti; still lifes of the common objects of a painter's studio—brushes, tubes, and cans of paint. The largest picture, and perhaps the finest, is of an orange grove, the whole canvas filled with leaves and fruit, relieved only in one corner by the tile roofing of a white-washed shed. Another, of a man and woman on a Vespa, illustrates brilliantly and touchingly how the scooter has motorized the love-life of Italy.

Guttuso is a fine painter. His compositions are free and emphatic. The color is perhaps more striking than harmonious. The vigor of his linear patterns, the bold opposition of colors, the constant presence of characterization carried almost to a caricature, give a poster-like projection. In fact, the work escapes the epithet "poster" only by the humanity of its conception and the sensitivity of the artist's hand. To make an arbitrary comparison, just as the work of Renoir is domestic and companionable, the work of Guttuso is public and moralistic.

Renoir was painting pictures designed for amateurs of painting living comfortable lives in comfortable houses. Consequently the works are soft and harmonious, subtle and detailed, made to be seen often and at close range. Guttuso, on the other hand, working in Italy, where there is little private collecting, paints for large exhibitions and museum purchase. The pictures are bold in design and color, striking in theme—with sociological overtones—and planned to read clearly from a distance. Pictures painted with this in mind must necessarily have more emphasis and less depth than more personalized work. And, though it is manifestly unfair to compare the living and the dead, Guttuso's brilliant manipulation of the declamatory style cannot be expected to offer as rich an experience as Renoir's quiet and confident serenity expressed through a more refined tradition.

# *Matta and David Smith*

THE MUSEUM of Modern Art is opening its fall season with two artists in the Surrealist tradition—the painter Matta and the sculptor David Smith. Smith works more like a blacksmith than like the conventional sculptor. He builds his pieces out of metal plates and bars, which he forges into shape and welds together. He employs a type of composition much in favor among his contemporaries wherein the sculpture is constructed as a cage, a framework, a skeleton, as an interlacing of struts rather than a continuous closed surface, the sculptor more concerned with the vacant spaces between the members than with the modeling of a surface or the mass inside a skin. This approach to composition has proved extremely useful to the abstract sculptors—both to the pure abstractionists like Calder or Pevsner who manipulate spatial relations or construct geometrical forms, as well as to the less severe Abstractionists like Smith himself whose work still retains some trace of Naturalistic subject matter.

Actually, abstraction comes much more easily to sculpture than to paint. The purely Abstract painter who eschews the aid of identifiable forms has great difficulty inventing means to depict a third dimension or to indicate a bulge or a recession in his picture. For the most part, he does not even attempt it, boasts virtuously that he is not violating the picture plane. Consequently, he is limited to working in flat shapes and linear patterns. The Abstract sculptor, on the other hand, has no trouble creating a third dimension. By the very nature of his materials the third dimension is already there, and the simple fact that his work can be viewed from every side gives it a kaleidoscopic multiplicity of geometrical relations and formal possibilities that abstract painting in flat pattern, even with all the resources of color, texture, and subliminal imagery, cannot approach.

Smith's own exposition is proof of this. The works done in the flat are much inferior to the others. The paintings and drawings, labyrinthine networks of dark on light, reminiscent of Arp or De Kooning, have little to hold the attention. The two small bas-reliefs, *Elements which Cause Prostitution* and *Chicago II,* are lumpish in form and naïve in modeling. But the objects made from fragments of metal welded together are varied and effective. Here, too, the sculptor has the advantage that he is using materials which, unlike paint or plasticine, have intrinsically beautiful textures. I particularly liked the *Australia,* a monstrous insect in thin metal rods; *The Royal Bird,* voracious and skeletal; the graceful *Leda* in steel plate; and the monumental *Sentinel III,* an upright construction of girder sections, conveniently mounted on wheels for easier mobility.

The paintings of Matta are perhaps not as weighty as this; they are certainly more entertaining, particularly the recent ones. The earlier works, those up into 1944, seem much less successful. The paint is less skillfully applied. The pigment is thin and greasy, put on with too much medium, the texture of the canvas always in evidence. The color has little invention or subtlety, most usually in vague tones of gray, brown or slate, accented with sudden explosions of magentas and electric greens. The drawing is soft and imprecise. The influences are quite evidently Max Ernst and Yves Tanguy, but without Ernst's variety and textures or Tanguy's precision and restraint. The general effect is of the colored plates of a medical dictionary seen out of focus.

The later paintings, on the other hand, are well painted, readable, and complex. The paint textures are firm, the color under control. Depth and recession are obtained by a very ingenious system of contour lines and overlapping rectangular planes seen in perspective, derived, perhaps, from the painting of Marcel Duchamp. Indeed one finds in one or two of these pictures something of the burnt-orange and olive tonality of Duchamp's *Descending Nude.* Most striking of all, the subject matter has changed. Instead of the imagery and associations of clinical biology we now find those of science fiction.

It is a menacing science fiction wherein appear the insectlike forms and the incomprehensible activities of beings from outer space: *Being With*—a pair of extraterrestrials, possibly male and female, travesties of mantis shape, performing on each other a series of unexplained and certainly painful operations in a geometrical setting which might be a Venusian laboratory or the interior of a cybernetics machine; *Against You: Dove Assassins*—in which white glider forms with mouths compactly filled with teeth swoop down upon the spectator; *The Spherical Roof Around Our Tribe*—which seems to depict the inside of a huge, transparent bubble where monstrous and alien beings press waiting against the outside of the glass; *The Unthinkable*—in which one creature, perhaps an artificial brain, is performing some sort of surgical experiment upon another. Whether or not one takes this seriously as painting, it is nonetheless vastly entertaining; an interstellar Mickey Mouse, the perfect illustrations for Clark's *Childhood's End,* a Disneylog of the measureless galactic spaces.

The element common to the two artists here on show is the constant use of the skeletal form, of the insect comparison. In David Smith the image seems to derive from the Picasso "bones," a series of pictures painted while Picasso was a member of the Surrealist Party. In Matta it would seem to come jointly from Dali's ants and Max Ernst's goblins, both painters at one time practicing Surrealists, as was Matta himself.

Surrealism in its original form was a literary movement based on the practice of automatic writing, the excessive metaphor derived from free association, the psychology of Freud, and the sociology of Trotsky. In the thirty's it offered directives to almost every art, from painting and poetry to interior decoration and portrait photography. Its chief canon was that art must be subversive, disquieting, and menacing.

To be disquieting and menacing is certainly the aim of the works here. In this they are not ineffective. Surrealism as a poetic discipline is now almost forgotten. But the threatening apparition as a subject for art—as in Max Ernst's demons, in Picasso's caricatures and monsters, or as one sees it here—is one element of the Surrealist conjuration which still retains its potency.

# *Miró*

A COMPREHENSIVE showing of the work of the Catalan Surrealist Joan Miró is on view at the Museum of Modern Art. It is apparently the most extensive exhibit of Miró's work ever assembled. The one hundred sixteen oils, prints, and sculptures present a review of the artist's entire production, from a canvas of 1914 to the illustrations of a book published only last year.

In comparison with Miró's familiar and established style, the early works seem unexpectedly labored and eclectic. The earliest ones, done in Spain, show all the modernist influences an up-and-coming young provincial painter would have been likely to encounter. The portraits recall Fauvism and Van Gogh. The landscapes, busy and detailed, are painstakingly executed in a hard-edged naturalism on which has been imposed a triangular segmentation like that of Severini and the other Italian Futurists. A *Seated*

*Nude* of 1919 is a laborious mixture of styles, the head rendered with a calendarlike prettiness, the body broken up into triangular planes in Futurist imitation, the pouf on which the model sits painted in hard naïve embroidery with roses. The three large still lifes of 1920 and 1921, done after the painter's arrival in Paris, derive their composition from those large vertical Cubist still lifes of Braque and Picasso in which the subject is a taboret with objects on it.

Despite the up-to-dateness of both subject and arrangement, the painting style of these early pictures is still a hard-edged, stylized Naturalism. *The Farm* of the following year is more characteristically Miró. It is a variation on the earlier Catalan landscapes, basically representational but made fanciful by the presence of tiny people and animals portrayed as grotesque and comic monsters—a mixture of peasant art, Fauvism, and the popular aspects of Cubism, curiously reminiscent of Baliev and his *Chauves Souris*. But these early pictures, more mannered even than Baliev, have a swarming complexity, as casually and cheerfully cruel as Catalan life itself.

Shortly after this, all trace of representation disappears from Miró's work, to be replaced by more advanced ideas. On his arrival in Paris in 1919 Miró had been introduced by the painter André Masson to the Dadaist group. Dada was then the newest and most exciting of the French intellectual movements, a violent and entertaining attack upon established literary and artistic values, a cult of nonsense, accident, and anti-reason. Typical examples of Dada art were the poems of Tristan Tzara composed by drawing the words one by one out of a sack, blindfolded; or the piece of sculpture submitted by Marcel Duchamp to an independent exhibition here (which refused it)—a cast-iron urinal, hung upside down, signed with a careful misspelling of the manufacturer's name, and entitled *Fountain*. The name Dada itself had been chosen because the word means something different in every language.

A system of logical unreason such as this is more useful as an instrument for public scandal than as a basis for artistic creation, and by 1923, Dada had already lost, along with its novelty and shock value, most of its reason for existence. André Breton revitalized it. He replaced Dada's subversive anti-intellectualism by the even more subversive systems of Freudian psychology and Communism. He restored its shock value with a highly advertised platform of cruelty —a cultivation of the sinister and obscure in human motivation quite different from Dada's amiable nonsense. He bound the members together with a discipline of free-association parlor games and psychological experimentation practiced as a rite, from Rorschach tests and hypnotism to essays in psychic domination and black magic. The group, essentially the same people as the Dadaists, reappeared in 1925 as the Surrealist—or Super-Realist party. And with Breton at its head as pope and arbiter, and with automatic writing as its characteristic working technique, it maintained the position for two decades as the strongest of all the power combines in the French artistic field.

Surrealism was essentially a literary movement, invented by poets and based on automatic word association and excessive metaphor. But like any artistic movement in France, it needed for its intellectual respectability the support of painters and was eager to take them in. It quickly acquired Dali, Masson, Tanguy, Valentine Hugo, Dominiguez, and others and engaged the support of many of the older generation like Picasso. How quickly Miró felt its influence can be seen in the *Tilled Field* of 1923-24—a year at least before the Surrealist party was officially announced—a picture painted without any attempt at representation and by the techniques of automatic association. Here, at length, Miró was at home. From this point on, the works may vary in detail; in style they do not change —a background in one plane on which are traced the curvilinear shapes which he invented, shapes which quickly replaced the Cubist triangle in interior decoration to become the common symbol, in ash trays, "free form" coffee tables, and even mobiles, of modernism in design. Note that the simple shapes and colors of the Calder mobiles had been used long before him by Miró. In Miró's work, however, one finds little of Calder's childlike good humor. They are too Barcelonese for that, gnomelike, busily witty, and coldly competent. Their semi-comic animals, microbe people, and schematized sex organs are mocking rather than gay, obsessive rather than companionable. On the other hand, their level of quality is so consistently high, each example so recognizably characteristic, each invariably what is called *un beau Miró*, that his work has been taken for the last twenty years as the common money of exchange on the Paris picture market, the ownership of a Miró being quite as good as a check in the bank.

The pictures here are handsome in texture and color and skillfully composed. Abstract as they may be, their intent is by no means decorative. Surrealism was not a technique for decoration. Its aim was subversion, its intent to undermine and dismay. And the Mirós, executed in strict accord with this unfriendly discipline, can end by being disturbing. I do not speak without cause; I have lived with them. A studio I rented in Paris in 1933 had a large one over the bed. I will not go so far as to claim that its malefic influence was what shortly sent me to a hospital with a foot infection. But I do know that after a month of sleeping in its company it had assumed such an unpleasant presence that—perhaps too late—I turned it to the wall.

And, having finished the rounds of the present exhibition, I was not at all sorry to leave for a breath of fresh air.

# *Hans Hofmann*

THE WHITNEY Museum is holding a retrospective exhibition of the German-born Hans Hofmann, veteran modern painter and most influential art teacher in America today. Most of the pictures shown were done during his long residence in this country. They are large and bright. The paint surface is thick and crusted, made up of impressive quantities of the most expensive pigments—pounds upon pounds of veridians, cadmiums, and cobalts, put on with brush, thumb, and palette knife. The forms portrayed are imprecise—patches and squiggles of vivid color in elaborately contrived textures. The titles are sometimes fanciful. The image is either negligible or non-existent. The work is direct and exuberant, with little wit, elegance, restraint, or tension—pure enthusiasm in paint.

Hofmann belongs among the Action painters, to the group otherwise known as the Abstract Expressionists. It is even likely that he is the inventor of the school, for most of its members in this country have been at one time his students. The ideas on which this school of painting is based have been somewhat obscured by its advocates, perhaps more intent on salesmanship than to clarity, but the ideas themselves are simple and respectable. They are roughly these:

It can be claimed with a great deal of reason that the beauty in a work of art comes from the pattern of shapes and colors on the canvas and from this alone; that our apprehension of this beauty has nothing to do with the objects these shapes and colors might depict or with the sentiments the depicted objects might evoke. Thus, the lift we feel in a Greco comes uniquely from the interlacing lines of its composition; the intense peace expressed in the face of a Cambodian Buddha is a question alone of the proportions and relations of its sculptured planes; and the impressive weight of a Cézanne still life comes only from the spatial relations of those solid chunks of depicted matter which, by habit and association, we name apples and pears. It can be furthermore claimed that the mere presence on the canvas of such objects or sentiments, by their very familiarity, obscures the real import of the picture. When these ideas first began to be taken seriously by teachers and painters some thirty years ago it was assumed that the basic structure of shape and color which constitutes beauty was a question of exact proportion, and probably had a numerical foundation. An esthetician named Hambidge revived a Renaissance tradition and suggested that beauty might be inherent in the incommensurable proportions of one-to-the-square-root-of-two, of-three, and of-five, and proceeded to derive the proportions of all Greek art and achitecture from one or another of these fundamental ratios. The idea is not impossible; to the Greeks these incommensurables, not being real like integers or fractions, probably seemed as divine and mysterious as beauty itself. At any rate, on this basis Hambidge and others proposed elaborate systems of dividing off the canvas, claiming thus to provide perfect compositions for the representational painter. The idea fitted Abstract painting even better; the Abstractionists took it over and their painting became more and more precise, with tight lines and sharply defined color areas. In most cases they did not follow a mathematical formula, but they believed, nevertheless, that the essence of beauty lay in the exact division of space and, in obedience to this notion, they tortured themselves to an almost Calvinistic exactitude.

A theory such as this eventually becomes untenable. It removes all freedom from the act of painting, and with the freedom goes also all the pleasure the painter takes in his labor. Another system had to be devised.

This was the present system of Abstract Expressionism, based principally, I believe, on certain early pictures of Kandinsky. The concept of the universe on which it is apparently based, I myself cannot accept. It is nonetheless quite tenable: that the cosmos is the result of accidents caused by chance encounters between energies; that the artist's mind is itself the result of similar accidents; and that if the painter surrenders to his subliminal motor impulses, the accidents his hand creates will automatically depict our accidental universe. This is the discipline of spontaneity—Abstract Expressionism's contribution to the technique of the art. With this discipline the abstract artist could imagine himself to be the instrument of forces greater than himself; his conscience was no longer racked by the demands of an impossible precision; his liberty of color and texture, so severely restricted under the tighter forms of abstraction, was restored to him, and he could again take pleasure in his work.

All the kinds of Abstract painting, however, have certain serious drawbacks. The principal one is that the picture tends to lie flat on the canvas. It is almost impossible for a painter who uses no images to obtain the illusion of depth or of space. Limited to surface pattern, the painting tends to become pure decoration. To overcome this limitation the Abstract painter frequently uses contrasts of hot and cold colors, claiming that by an optical illusion, the red will advance from the picture plane and the blue will retreat into it, and thus provide his picture with a third dimension. The effect is very marked if one uses red and blue lights. But when dealing with pigments instead of lights, despite the confidence Cézanne himself had in the theory, the effect is so slight as to be almost negligible. To achieve depth, the abstract painter can also take advantage of tones and values. Any irregular mottling when looked at with the eye of the imagination will give bulges and recesses, heads and landscapes. But in a purely Abstract picture, such variations of depth are placed there by the fancy of the spectator and not by the design of the painter. In principle, Abstract painting is severely two dimensional, and I do not at all understand the apologists who speak so fervently of these painters' "exploration of space."

Disciplines of painting such as the two I have described tend to form schools. It is perhaps more accurate to say that these disciplines are the product of schools. Certainly they are more useful to teaching and industry than to the independent artists. I suspect that the independent artist, once his student days are over, finds their possibilities too limited. They confine him to the exploitation of shapes and colors, to the elaboration of textures, to the exploration of his own motor impulses. He is forced inside himself, cut off from the fecundation he might find in the outside world, limited to decoration—or to anti-decoration—and forbidden the expression of personal poetry.

The present exhibition shows little that is personal. It is all virtuosity. It is exuberant and noncommittal in the highest possible key. It is like a classroom demonstration by an overbrilliant teacher —all that cannot easily be taught has been avoided. Hofmann has always taught, has always been surrounded by the admiration of students. That is perhaps why his work seems more the expression of a cult than a serious attack on the problems of artistic communication.

# *Leonid*

TWENTY-FIVE new landscapes by Leonid are on view at Durlacher—principally scenes from the rice fields of Asia and the clam flats of New England. The paint is dry and a little powdery, the colors pale and nacreous, the texture matte. The whole effect is gouache-like and luminous. The New England pictures follow Leonid's more familiar pattern of great horizontal stretches of sky and beach. More unusual for him are his Tuscany farm lands, and his Manila rice fields with their severe geometrical perspective and native laborers in angular costumes. The finest are two vertical zigzag compositions painted as if seen from somewhat above—the one a floating tangle of Bangkok market rafts, the other a string of Philippine fishermen lined up on a tidal flat casting their circular hand nets—as easy, charming, and exotic as a *chinoiserie* by Pillement, though certainly more serious as to painting.

Marshes and beaches are Leonid's characteristic subject. For him the edges of the sea are neither vacation land nor stage. He sees them rather as a vast and aqueous farm, intensely cultivated, each of whose products—the oyster, the mussel, the seaweed used for fertilizer—serves him in turn as the theme for a series of pictures whose elements are the weather, tides, geography, people, and particular methods of cultivation, and whose basic subject matter could be described in the language of science as the riparian ecology of man.

No one is as skillful as Leonid in aerial perspective—in making things retreat into the distance by painting the intervening air; his landscapes extend miles into the canvas. And no one knows as well as he how to seize the color of light and sky peculiar to each place. But despite their air of specific accuracy, the pictures are not, as in Impressionist painting, views of particular places taken, like a photograph, from a particular spot. They are generalizations, not painted from nature, but done in the studio from memory. This non-Impressionist approach, like that of any classical landscape painter of the seventeenth or eighteenth century, is the one characteristic Leonid holds in common with that highly diversified band, the Neo-Romantics, of which he is an important member.

The Neo-Romantic painters first appeared in 1926 in Paris as a group exposition at the Galerie Drouet. The band consisted of Christian Bérard, the Dutchman Christians Tonny, the Russian Pavel Tchelitchew, Leonid and his brother Eugène Berman, and, for a short time, Pierre Charbonier and Therèse Debains. The name Neo-Romantic was invented by the critic Waldemar George to describe the introspective quality of their work. The styles and subject matter of no two were alike; all that united them was their youth and talent and a common revolt against the already congealed and academicized Cubist movement.

In their search for a more sensitive depiction of their own times, the Neo-Romantics went back to Picasso's early blue period with its preoccupation with the "poor in spirit" while Eugène Berman and Leonid devoted themselves to the moody aspects of ruins and nature. All carefuly avoided any reference to the prosperous externals of middle-class life. Their pictures were for the most part dark, influenced in tone and color by the blue-period Picassos. The essential mood of the work, to use Cocteau's word for it, was "mystère," which appears as a common characteristic of the people in the pictures—relaxed but not placid, self-contained, and eternally untouched by the news of the day. The subject of each painter was a personal poetry. Bérard painted large, uncharacterized portrait heads which somehow managed in their intense intimacy to express a tenderness for all humanity. Tchelitchew, through his still lifes of oversized eggs and his Siamese-twinlike human bodies and doubled faces, conveyed a glimpse of the restless sensuality underlying all nature. Berman's night scenes of quay-side stock piles gave a concrete image of loneliness, Tonny's drawings—Neo-Romantic only in that they were imaginative and in no way abstract or Impressionist—of hordes and battles of insect creatures, showed him to be a sort of modern Bosch, nearest of all the group to the Surrealists but without Surrealism's essential malice. Leonid himself painted very much as today—boats and marines in muted colors, the compositions corrected in the studio according to the pre-Impressionist rules of art.

From the mid-twenties until the war, Neo-Romanticism and its bitter rival Surrealism were the only two schools of painting to oppose the triumphant progress of Abstraction. Both were schools of poetic painting and for the most part were representational. Apart from that, the two movements were unlike in every way. Neo-Romanticism was politically indifferent and sociologically compassionate. Its subject matter was the personal sentiments of the painter about persons and places. Surrealism, on the other hand, was Marxian in politics, with a subject matter derived from psychoanalytic theory with subversive intent added. Surrealism, though essentially literary rather than a painting movement, proved the stronger. It was commercially better organized and its aggressive doctrines had a wider intellectual appeal than Neo-Romanticism's more private-minded dependence on individual sensitivity. Surrealism's working methods of automatic association were adopted by painters not connected with the movement, and the suggestive imagery it invented has enormous success in commercial art. Dali, its principal painter (popularly considered a Surrealist long after he had been expelled from the group), having mastered advertising, attempted as well the conquest of the stage. But his ballet designs and costumes, though striking, were too eccentric to establish an acceptable style. On the other hand, the stage designs of Bérard, Tchelitchew, and Berman were the finest of our time. Bérard was also responsible for much of the Second Empire revival in interior decoration that was characteristic of the thirties, and his drawings and ideas for costume design not only set the women's fashions of his time, but later formed the basis for the world-wide success of the dressmaking firm of Christian Dior.

As a movement in painting, Neo-Romanticism was less successful. It attracted a few new adherents and, like so much work based on youthful lyricism, it lost all too quickly its original tension and purity. Bérard who was its leader in France was never able to achieve the position in French painting his great talent and intelligence seemed to promise. Perhaps because of indolence, perhaps because his energies were dissipated by opium and high society, he produced many fine beginnings but disappointingly few works finished and important enough to sustain his reputation. Tchelitchew was the finest draftsman since Ingres. Nonetheless, all but his earliest work, which is in rich grays and blacks only, suffers apparently from a superficial understanding of color. And many of his later works, in addition to their garishness, have an unquiet and unfortunate elaboration, all too obviously due to Surrealistic influence. Eugène Berman, less forceful perhaps as a draftsman, but a much richer painter, also shows in much of his later work a taste for restless complexities. This is however probably less due to Surrealist influence than to diligence of mind.

Of all these painters, Leonid is the only one who has never touched the theater. Also, like Bérard, he has never been influenced in any way by Surrealism or other movements in literature or politics. Nor has he experimented much with pen, pencil, gouache or portraiture. His constant adherence to the kind of subject matter he finds personally inspiring and his unswerving devotion to oil paint have enabled him to produce a body of work remarkably sustained in quality. And it is undoubtedly due to this singleness of aim that one finds in the present show the same subtle light and convincing poetry that have always rendered his pictures so enchanting.

# *Portraits — Annigoni, Eakins, Bouché, Rivers*

THE FIRST American showing, at Wildenstein's, of the work of Pietro Annigoni, said to be the most expensive portrait painter of our day; the exhibition of Thomas Eakins at the American Academy of Arts and Letters; René Bouché's portraits of international celebrities on view at the Iolas Gallery; and the group of portraits by Larry Rivers at the Tibor de Nagy—taken all together, bring up an old troublesome question—when is a portrait a work of art?

The Annigonis are sumptuous and carefully executed. The painter demands, I understand, some thirty-five hours of pose. Their general manner is reminiscent of Holbein and of early Renaissance—the forms handsomely modeled in the round, the painting detailed and smooth. The medium, which is something of a mystery, is apparently a water-thinned tempera emulsion applied between layers of varnish, the ground being a rag paper mounted on canvas. The surface of the smaller works is glossy and mechanically perfect, like the handworked finish of an expensive car. The drawing is subtle, direct, and skillful. The color is rich but not particularly interesting.

Annigoni's technical mastery is astonishing, but the results seem both ostentatious and servile. He does not attempt to prettify his sitters; he is too sound a draftsman for that. He flatters nonetheless by attributing to his sitters an intense emotional life. He neglects their real and possibly less showy character to depict them as if possessed by sentimental memories and amorous anticipations. The most striking example of this is in his portrait of the present Queen of England, posed on a hill against the sky, her eye illuminated by the light of love, like any actress in a singing movie.

Thomas Eakins was technically much less competent. As a portrait painter he was incomparably more manly. As one can see in the forty-six pictures on display, his work is very uneven. The painting is heavy and laborious. His handling, learned under Gerôme at the École des Beaux Arts, with its opaque darks and loaded and somewhat greasy lights, has little ease. Details are often overworked at the expense of the general form and pattern. The pictures are often overlarge, their empty compositions incredibly naïve. (Witness the portrait of Riter FitzGerald, an amiable life-sized gentleman seated in a huge square canvas three-quarters filled with books in bookcases.) The landscapes and many of the genre pictures have quite wonderful color, but the greater number of the interiors, with their heavy shadows and dull tones, convey the unhappy impression of having been painted at night by gaslight. The painting is forceful; it is not handsome. One thinks of Eakins as an industrious and clumsy man, hampered by the limitations of an inferior tradition, but who by the force of his stubbornness and honesty arrived at painting unforgettable pictures.

Certainly the portraits are unforgettable. There is no stylization whatsoever of the subjects' character, no attempt to make them more winning or comely. They are given no artificial grandeur. The men are heavy, ugly, and pleased to be painted. Walt Whitman appears as what he most probably was, a perfect likeness to the king in *Huckleberry Finn.* The women are more interesting—serious, strong, competent, seen in the round. Their portraits are among his most successful pictures—*Katherine,* playing with her cat, *Miss Amelia C. Van Bureau, The Pathetic Song*—fine portraits and fine painting as well. But even in his inferior pictures he kept his professional dignity. He tried to please no one but himself.

The painting of René Bouché is witty, brilliant, and civilized. He is more acute than Annigoni and more superficial than Eakins by the very nature of his sitters, who—Georges Braque, Jean Cocteau, Mlle. Chanel, Mme. Claude Alphand, Christian Dior, Truman Capote, Aldous Huxley—are princes and princesses of the international world of fashion. Bouché's color is brilliant, his paint thin and fluid, his execution nervous and accurate, in the soundest virtuoso tradition of our time—straight from the Fauves, from Van Dongen, Bérard, and Dufy.

The canvases are large enough to give the painter ease, but not unwieldy. The arrangements of the sitters against their characteristic background—Chanel at home, Dior at dinner—could not be more ingenious or successful. But the most striking thing about these portraits is that the sitters are presented from the outside. We see them as if at an afternoon party—well dressed, self-possessed, amiable enough, and at their right age. The painter has kept his distance. This complete detachment is the work's greatest elegance. The limitation this attitude imposes on the painter's vision is also perhaps its weakness.

Perhaps not. Bouché's sitters belong to a class known to publicity and to the stage as "the big time." The distinguishing mark of this class is a firm and easily projected personality, recognizable and uniform, without visible reticences or contradictions. It is evidence of Bouché's strength that he has been able to present the fabulous masks of these perhaps most mythical creatures of our time without either adulation or resentment. It is also evidence of his sensitivity that he occasionally allows himself to reveal more—as in his portrait of Cocteau, where one may glimpse behind the mask an aged and embittered eagle.

Bouché's painting method is improvisation. The pictures are

done directly from the subject in two or three sittings, and not retouched afterward, the only preparation being a sitting or so of rapid pencil drawings whose purpose is to introduce the model to his painter. With Larry Rivers, improvisation is carried still further. There is no preparation whatsoever. The sitter is painted directly on the canvas in a series of sketches in full color. The successive sketches are not superimposed as is ordinarily the case in painting, where each day's work corrects or completes the work of the preceding sitting. Instead they are spread over the canvas in the manner of an album leaf. The individual studies are never carried to completion, but the conjunction of their various details presents a kaleidoscopic and surprisingly convincing image of the sitter. (Particularly successful in this are the two portraits of the artist's son, *Stevie in a Plaster Cast* and *Stevie on Crutches,* each with its seven or eight unfinished depictions.) The canvases are relatively large to give room for this multiplied image. The colors are light and gay, the great areas of exposed ground serving to define the general picture tone. The line quality is less sensitive and less expressive than Bouché's, the pictures more anecdotal and private. They present a history of the painter's relation to his sitter rather than a formalized resemblance. But they are in no way hermetic; they are only incompletely stated. Their very incompletion gives them a charm and a continuing interest that more labored work might not possess.

The four painters here are strikingly different in character. The works of Annigoni are above all rich, of Eakins honest, of Rivers spontaneous, and of Bouché intelligent. But what could be the particular quality which would give survival value to work whose only theme is a human resemblance?

It might be that quality in the painter himself which combines professional pride and moral responsibility. The unique aim of the painter's training has been to teach him to see. This ability constitutes his professional qualification. He can see better than anyone else and what he sees is what the world of his time looks like. If his portrait is to be a respectable professional performance and capable of interesting a later time, it must depict what the painter sees, not what the sitter imposes. Any concession, any flattery, any undeserved attribution of charm, beauty, majesty, what you will, however reassuring it may be to a client, lessens the portrait as a work of art. Because, in the long run, a work of art presents only the likeness of its maker. This is why the painting of Annigoni, in spite of his superb technical mastery, remains modish and frivolous, and why the work of Eakins, a provincial painter schooled in what was probably the worst tradition of painting the world has ever known, is impossible to forget. As a professional, Eakins was a proud man.

# *Winslow Homer*

THE WINSLOW Homer retrospective, organized by the National Gallery of Washington, has arrived in New York to be shown at the Metropolitan. There are seventy-nine oils, more than a hundred water colors and numerous drawings and prints—the most comprehensive show of Homer ever given. The work ranges from a *Harper's Weekly* illustration of 1859, when the artist was twenty-three, to a canvas, *Shooting the Rapids, Saguenay River,* left unfinished at his death in 1910.

Homer's work divides into two distinct periods. First is the work done before his trip to England in 1881—scenes from American farm, soldier, and summer life, executed principally in oil. The pictures of the second period have for subject the landscape and seacoasts of Maine and the West Indies. Here the finest and most original part is in water color.

The work done before 1881 is not very different, even in scale, from the other American nineteenth-century genre painting, though it seldom arrives at being as finished or unified as that of Mount or Bingham. The color, however, is invariably more interesting—incisive, rich, and for the most part surprisingly dark. The subjects are commonplace and rural—children in a catboat or taking cows to pasture, girls walking on a beach or playing croquet—so commonplace that even Henry James, reporting an exhibition, complained of a "pie-nurtured maiden" and "blankness of fancy" and called the work honest and manly but "damnably ugly." However, it is in large part due to these now-vanished commonplaces that the work today has its extraordinary charm.

In these youthful pictures the faces are frequently over-detailed —the result, one supposes, of Homer's training as an illustrator, and a few of the works (*Morning Glories* of 1873 for example— a young woman in a window framed with climbing plants) are as inept and sentimental as a commercial lithograph. Most, however, are very much alive and the best are extraordinarily fine: *On The Beach*, for one, with its majestic rollers sweeping in, and in one corner tiny figures of ladies wading, obviously summer visitors, with comically fat legs; or *East Hampton, Long Island* of 1874, with its girls under beach parasols in the Atlantic summer light. This last, in crispness of tone, placement, and painting, is as good as the best of Boudin. The final oil of this period is one of his most remarkable—*The Campfire* of 1880—the woods at night with two hunters around a fire, in which the column of ascending sparks is a *tour de force*—as astonishing as some of the effects of Rubens.

From this point on the oils become heavier and emptier—quite as anecdotal as the illustrations to the popular novels of the times and in every way less engaging. There are, of course, exceptions. *The Hound and Hunter* of 1892, for example—a young Indian guide (probably a real person; he appears in several other pictures) being towed in his canoe by a swimming stag and warning off his dog—is an admirable picture. But the monumental English fisher maids, and even the thundering Maine Coast scenes of these later years seem tiresome and dated. The water colors, on the contrary, are freer, more spontaneous and economical than before, and constantly surprise with their variety, subtlety and skill.

Water color, used as one finds it here to make a finished picture, seems to have been a late nineteenth-century—and probably English—invention. Earlier water colors—by Turner, Delacroix, and even as late as those of Cézanne—were generally either notations of ideas or sketches for pictures. The water color as an end in itself, as well as the brilliant technique we ourselves associate with the medium, came I think from the introduction of a new sort of water-color paper, known as "cold pressed." This, a heavy, heavily sized, rough, rag paper, will not accept the detailed drawing necessary in a painter's working sketches. But its tough surface is not so easily marred by erasure as the lighter paper formerly in use. And the English painters found that its heavy substance, once wet, would, in their damp climate, stay wet for hours. In this state it permitted all sorts of hazy, misty softnesses and pictorial atmospheric effects. (Look, for example, at Homer's *Houses of Parliament* in the present show, done on this rough paper and in the English climate.) The effects were so satisfactory and characteristic that water color began to be commonly practiced as an end in itself.

In a drier climate, however, the technique is impractical. The paper dries too soon. And another technique was devised, perhaps by Homer himself, which afterwards became the standard practice—of painting on the paper, but without wetting it, in broad, crisp washes, put down as directly as possible and allowed to dry untouched, the painter using no other white than the white of the paper itself. This is the exact opposite to painting in oil, where white is the most important of the pigments, where work done *à premier coup* is likely to seem dead, and where paint quality must be achieved by many layers one on top of the other. The two techniques are in fact so different that when a painter becomes expert in one, he seldom maintains his skill or interest in the other. This is probably what happened to Homer's later oils.

The work in the show is somewhat uneven as is inevitable in an artist with two such contrary sides—of provincial professional illustrator and knowledgeable Impressionist. But all the finest pieces are here, and even the lesser ones have something of that dramatic sense of color, that accurate feeling for people, places, times, light, and weather, which make Homer one of the best loved painters of our country.

## *Eilshemius*

FORTY OILS of Louis Eilshemius are on view at The Artists' Gallery. Eilshemius, or as he preferred to call himself, "Dr. Louis M. Eilshemius, M.A., etc.," followed with painful exactitude the life of the great and misunderstood artist of romantic literature. Born in New Jersey in 1864 of prosperous parents, he had every advantage of education and travel—in Germany, this country, Paris, Africa, and the South Seas. He painted diligently and in complete obscurity until 1917 when, at the age of fifty-three, he was suddenly "discovered." The price asked for his picture in that year's Independent show caught Marcel Duchamp's eye. The magnificent nerve of a completely unknown painter demanding $6,000 for a not very good picture (the *Rose-Marie* of the present show) at a time when a good Cézanne could be had for $600 struck Duchamp's acute sense of the absurd. He sought the painter out and found a quiet little man who soberly and reasonably explained that he, Eilshemius, was the foremost genius of the age—a painter greater than Rembrandt, a musician greater than Beethoven, a writer who combined the gifts of Shakespeare with those of Byron. He had painted thousands of pictures (there are more than thirty-five hundred oils extant and innumerable drawings and water colors), he had written some two hundred musical compositions and three hundred volumes of poems and stories, and all this at top speed: at the rate of forty-five minutes for a painting, three hours for a short story, and sonnets on the average of three minutes each. He carried in his pocket a pamphlet which recounted his accomplishments:

> Educator, ex-actor, amateur all-around doctor, mesmerist-prophet and mystic, reader of hands and faces, linguist of five languages, graphologist, dramatist (seven works), short story writer and novelettes (twenty-six works), humorist galore, ex-mimic (animal voices and humans), ex-all-around athlete sportsman (to 1889), universal supreme critic, ex-Don Giovanni [perhaps in reference to a method he had devised for attracting women which involved a fixed stare and a pendulum-like motion of the head], designer of jewelry, etc.; spiritist, spirit-painter supreme. . . .

And so on for three more paragraphs.

Duchamp, himself a prime mover in the Dada movements, a very Leonardo of the logic and mechanics of nonsense, must have found such immoderate self-esteem extremely gratifying. And just as the satirist Alfred Jarry, author of *Ubu Roi,* had been amused by the Douanier Rousseau's zany character, and instigated his launching, so Duchamp instigated the launching of the much more extravagant Eilshemius. At any rate, in 1920 the Societé Anonyme, founded by Duchamp and Katherine Drier, staged Eilshemius' first one-man show. This had no success whatever, and in 1921 Eilshemius, discouraged, gave up painting for good. Presently, however, the pictures, which had all been acquired by dealers for little or nothing, began to sell. None of this profited the painter who, having come to the end of his resources, was living in debt and poverty. By 1939, the contrast between the painter's extreme indigence and the sums his pictures were bringing the dealers had become so scandalous that Juliana Force of the Whitney Museum organized a committee to come to his aid. He died two years later at the age of seventy-seven, poor, embittered, famous, and probably mad. As an edifying and fitting end to the story, his funeral was attended by all the most famous figures in American art.

Seen thirty years later, the pictures are less edifying. In fact they are disappointing—so uneven and hasty that it is almost cruel to judge them by ordinary professional standards. Their general style is that of the wall decorations in Italian-American restaurants. The color is pallid and sometimes charming. Some of the landscapes, the less romantic ones, have considerable air and distance. The Romanticism of the subject matter is for the most part childish and the figure compositions are more than inept. The nudes and figures are of the standard type to be found in the figure drawing of those elderly ladies and gentlemen who attend life-class as a hobby and who will never improve—with tiny hands and feet, ball-like breasts, and heads with hair and features carefully assigned. Some few of the pictures, nevertheless, possess a naïve charm which goes far to explain his popularity.

Eilshemius, however, was not a naïve painter: he was an ignorant one, a painter who had attended all the schools and yet had never succeeded in learning the basic lesson of how to see. Learning takes a certain humility, all too difficult for one accustomed to call himself "the Supreme Parnassian and Grand Transcendent Eagle of Arts." It has been suggested that Eilshemius' complex egotism made difficult his recognition as a painter. That is not likely. Very little of the painting is that good. Except for the extravagances of his megalomania, he would probably not have been discovered at all.

# SECOND THOUGHTS

# *Art and Murals*

VERY LITTLE mural painting is commissioned in our day. One wonders why. The blank walls of our severe contemporary buildings cry out for decoration. The owners are certainly rich enough to pay for it, and we have plenty of painters around. The difficulty, I suspect, is subject matter. Nobody can think of a story worth while painting.

In a finished picture subject matter does not seem very important. It tends to disappear behind the much more striking idiosyncracies of the painter's style. A picture of a countess and a prostitute differ principally for the spectator in that one is by Degas and the other by Toulouse-Lautrec. Nevertheless, the two simple notions—that one of these ladies was respectable and the other was not—were the generating ideas which made the pictures possible.

Subject matter in this sense—something that interests the painter enough to keep him on his toes and at his best throughout his labor—is particularly difficult in the case of mural painting. Here the subject must be broad enough to interest a great many people and at the same time complex and personal enough to inspire the painter. In the past the stories of Christian iconography, royal grandeurs, and pagan myth furnished neutral subject matter, interesting to everybody, and accepting from the painter any amount of elaboration. The stories embodied a way of thinking normal to the time. The painter was expected to illustrate and embroider, not to convince.

Today, the subjects found fecund in the past give us much trouble. Commerce and industry, the life of Christ, the pleasures of middle-class life (so productive for the Impressionists), the noble workman, the history of our country, or the statement of a political creed —none of these is neutral any longer. Enlarged to the size of the walls of a public building, they tend to become a form of advertising instead of painting.

Some painting of this sort was attempted in this country under the WPA. As we all remember, it generally took as subject some mild form of political or social betterment and proved to be so completely without interest that almost no mural painting has been seen here since. There has also been a great deal of mural painting of this order in Mexico during the last three decades. But these pictures can scarcely be called real painting. With their simplicities and violences, they are rather examples of the political poster, and are as out of place in contemporary achitecture as would be the shallow optimism of our highway billboards.

It is all, I think, a question of the painter's sincerity. With these impersonal generalizations as subject matter the painter finds himself doing a form of commercial art. He is illustrating ideas which he has reason to believe are approved of by his client. He is addressing himself not to his client, but to a vague entity he knows only as his client's public, and he must do this using his client's words. Whereas real painting, to have any sort of integrity, must be painted about things which interest the painter himself.

Consequently, a good mural painting in the past has always been a large picture of the things the painter liked to paint, and differed from his easel pictures only in size, visibility at a distance, and scale. Modern architecture would be satisfied with pictures such as these. But large pictures in the representational style, painted of something which was of personal interest to the painter, are rare and very expensive. Since large pictures with subject matter have proved so difficult, contemporary architects, in recent years, have sought to decorate their buildings with paintings in the abstract style having as little subject matter as possible. Unfortunately, until recently the only abstract style available for these murals has been the style out of which modern architecture itself derives—the straight-line cutouts of the Bauhaus, the cylindrical forms of Léger or the dry rectangles of Mondrian—all that would seem most rigid and dehumanized in modern art. This does not work well at all. Modern architecture needs as a relief from its own severity something with a great deal more ease and freedom.

This need is satisfied, I believe, by the painters grouped under the name of Abstract Expressionists. The school has many adherents both here and abroad. Pollock, De Kooning, Rothko, Mathieu are a few that come to mind. They are reputed the most revolutionary of present-day painters. Judging from the work itself, this reputation seems excessive since the canons they follow are today relatively conservative. They appear to form an academy of eclectic Modernism, seeking to combine in their pictures—as did the Academy of Bologna—the best qualities of the painters they most admire: in this case Miró, Klee, and Kandinsky instead of Leonardo, Michelangelo, and Raphael. They employ as a rigorous working method the automatic techniques—the disciplines of spontaneity and non-meaning—akin to the technique of automatic writing used by some modern poets, and which certainly can be called academic, since it is taught today in all the schools. The most striking characteristics of these painters' work are the large size of their canvases and their systematic use of the accidents, the drips, runs, and spatters which can happen in applying wet paint to a surface.

The pictures of these Abstract Expressionists suit admirably the modern buildings. They are large, free in execution, decorative, and completely without embarrassment of subject matter. There is no story to be illustrated, no meaning the spectator can be asked to comprehend. Their subject matter—in spite of the punning, poetic, or divergent titles the pictures frequently exhibit, and in spite of the somewhat obscure philosophizing with which the school is promoted—is the paint surface of the picture itself. The freedom and variety of this surface marries perfectly with the habitual severity of contemporary architecture. The relative excellence of one of these pictures is easy to determine, for it depends entirely on the beauty of shapes, colors, textures, and their arrangement. There is no trouble about scale; the pictures can be executed as large as needed without excessive effort on the painter's part. In short, this school has probably produced the most useful style of wall decoration yet to appear in our century.

But, however useful this work may be, and however brilliant a future I believe is in store for it, I must nevertheless insist that it belongs among the applied and not among the fine arts. Real painting has two characteristics which these pictures do not possess—it exploits a third dimension and it communicates ideas.

Painting is not the work of a solipsist. The painter acts as if he were one of Leibnitz's monads, reflecting all the other elements in the universe. As Manet said: the painter is an eye. He is a conscious being living in a spatial world. The drama and the tension of his painting comes from this duality: of the outside world in which he moves, and the inner world within his mind which feels, distorts, rejects, and chooses. The painter who shuts himself off from the outside world ignores its extension in space and its emotional and motor connotations, must limit his subject matter to the visceral tensions, his images to the sexual symbols, and his art itself to an inappropriate imitation of the art of music.

It must be admitted that a great deal of Abstract Expressionism's success as decoration comes from its careful avoidance of all communication. The egg-and-dart, the Greek key, the Persian pomegranate could not be used as decorative motifs until they had lost their original ceremonial meanings; the shape of an Oriental script seems pretty to us because we do not know what it means. Nevertheless, pure decoration is something painters have always sought to avoid. Picasso himself, quite early in his career, abandoned strict Cubism because it seemed to lead to decoration, and, to keep his pictures in the realm of legitimate painting, took to using recognizable subject matter. This, however, the Abstract Expressionists will not do. Their unrelieved loyalty to the discipline of non-meaning renders them incapable of communicating a visual idea, or even of transmitting a personal emotion. I am aware that the artist who uses these automatic techniques is frequently convinced that his work is heavy with meaning. But these are meanings which do not communicate and which, at their clearest, express only the vast banalities of the unconscious mind.

As for the other quality which distinguishes real painting—the use of a third dimension—all appearance of depth or of solid form is so consistently absent that one is frequently led to suspect that the painters have been insufficiently trained. This, I know, is not true of De Kooning, and may be a willful affection on the part of the other painters as well. Nevertheless, their firm refusal to render space, to depict a world, or to communicate an idea, whether it be from caprice or necessity, removes them from among the painters and places them among the decorators and artisans.

But this has little to do with the matter at hand. The painters are skillful, inventive, and sensitive. Their work is professional, useful, and varied. The elements out of which it is made are well known and everywhere accepted. The publicity which promotes the school is controversial, asserting, as it does, that these painters are the bearers of some obscure and portentious message. But the pictures themselves are not controversial in any way. Once their immense value as decoration is admitted, and their negligible interest as poetry is avowed, the public resistance to these painters can only disappear and their work will receive the wide employment it so well deserves.

# *Whitney and the Institute*

THE WHITNEY Museum is holding a show of thirty American painters and sculptors, under thirty-five, and representative of present-day trends. Last month the National Institute of Arts and Letters exhibited the work of thirty-five artists chosen by the painter and sculptor members of the Institute as applicants for the

Institute's annual grants. Both shows were drawn from the same pool of contemporary artists, but were chosen according to different points of view.

The selecting committee for the Whitney show, on the one hand, contains no artists. And since the Whitney Museum is extremely sensitive to present-day critical currents, and closely associated with the educational program of the Museum of Modern Art, the show it offers can be taken to represent the advanced critical and academic opinion—an official view of American contemporary painting from outside the profession.

The selecting body of the Institute, on the other hand, consists entirely of artists. Its choice represented another view of the same field, but this time from within. The two views have very little in common.

The Whitney's is the more arresting. Certainly its show is the more violent, due to the number of pictures whose theme is caricature and to the quantity of large, bright, non-objective pictures in the "action painting" style. The theory behind action painting, as it has been explained to me, is this: The real subject of a picture is not, as one generally thinks, a visual idea. The real subject is the muscular pleasure the painter takes in the unhampered motion of his brush. The spectator's pleasure in the resulting picture comes from his sympathetic motor responses to the bodily movements of the painter recorded in the brush strokes. Consequently, action pictures must be large—to give the painter space for large and ample movements (this must be what the apologists for these severely two-dimensional canvases mean when they praise the painter's "exploration of space")—and the paint put on must be heavy. In the present show, of the twenty-four painters represented, thirteen lie somewhere within this category, eight in that of caricature, one is a pure Abstractionist, and two have a Naturalistic subject matter, these figures including several borderline cases.

One has the impression that the pictures of the Whitney show have been chosen from considerations of visibility rather than of subtlety, of wit rather than of visual idea, of brushwork rather than of color, of initial impact rather than of memorability. But this is to be expected. Brushwork, visibility, and wit in painting, like skillful orchestration in music, can be recognized at once by any committee. Whereas subtlety of composition, harmony of color, and interest of visual idea, like the beauty of a melodic line, take a certain amount of living with to be appreciated.

Among the most interesting of the non-Objective paintings are those by John Levee—layer upon layer of creamy paint in rich, harmonious colors—and by Paul Jenkins, whose decorative canvases resemble enlargements of the polished cross section of a mineral. Gerald McLaughlin, whom I place among the caricaturists, is perhaps the most entertaining. His cities (or battles or mob scenes, as you will) of tiny monsters—potato-like shapes, phallic and wiggling—are fascinating and appalling, and beautifully executed. Among the sculptors the expressions of caricature are on the whole more interesting and skillful than the abstract work displayed. Witness Elbert Weinberg with his *Procession* of life-size rabbis in full regalia, Richard Stankiewicz with his personages welded together of old machine parts, and Paul Frazier, with his handsome *Dog Trying to Go to Heaven.*

Except for action painting, caricature, and their intermixture, there is not much of interest. The one pure Abstractionist shown is thin and trite, and of the two representational painters who do not employ caricature, one is weak and the other inept and overambitious.

In the work at the Institute, on the other hand, caricature is almost entirely absent, and the opposition of caricature and brilliance of paint texture in no way stressed. One finds instead the opposition which is most interesting to a jury of painters, that age-old problem of the Painter and his Model—the opposition of style and subject matter.

I am sure that no one who does not paint himself can possibly understand the importance a painter gives to subject matter. Subject matter, even if in the end it is entirely eliminated from the picture, is the germ which has engendered the whole work. And as for style, stylization to a painter is almost synonymous with the act of painting itself. It is how the subject is to be got on canvas. So that it is not surprising that the pictures of this show, chosen by a jury of painters, range from the Naturalistic to complete Abstraction, with all the gradations between.

The show here is not as brilliant as the Whitney's. It is more uneven. But it has greater variety and contains a greater number of individually interesting pictures. The Abstract works of Paul Burlin, John Von Wicht, and Kenzo Okada (whom I suppose to be classed among the action painters) are finer by far in color and in general elegance than corresponding pictures at the Whitney. A painter jury is apt to have a good eye. And the one painter present in both expositions, Jonah Kinigstein, is represented here by much better pictures, in particular by a *Sicilian Altar,* with the saint glittering and dripping with candlelight and gold, more accomplished than anything of his the Whitney shows. A work by Joe Lasker especially sticks in the mind: *Naples,* loaned by the Whitney, a composite view of the city done in the colors and textures of a Pompeian fresco.

A group exposition is almost bound to be a portrait of the jury that chose the pictures. A non-painting jury will select what it considers to combine the most striking with the most up-to-date. The most striking qualities today would appear to be violence and caricature. The artist jury selects pictures that it considers to offer contemporary solutions to the problem always facing the artist—the problem of presenting an idea in visual terms.

Both exhibitions contain many fine works. Their common weakness lies in the frequent exploitation of tricks—tricks of air brush, knife, spatter and drip, formulas of drawing and of stylistic evocation—employed more for their own sake than for any useful expressive purpose. The insistent presence of tricks such as these is precisely what gives both shows their "official" aspect. For, just as we slight-ingly apply "academic" to painting which pays undue reverence to things learned at school, so "official" has come to imply the incontinent exploitation of fashionable novelty.

# *Nature in Abstraction, and Louis Comfort Tiffany*

UNDER THE general title of Nature in Abstraction, the Whitney Museum is holding an exhibit of fifty-eight American paintings and sculptures, for the most part by Abstract Expressionists. The works are colorful, noncommittal, scrupulously individualized, and singularly unsurprising, being by the same group of painters appearing in every Whitney show and in every issue of *The Arts* and *Art Digest*. The greatest novelty lies in the exhibition's name, taken because—as Mr. John I. H. Baur, curator of the museum, explains in his preface to the handsome catalogue—these painters, without ceasing to be abstract, are now beginning to take their themes from nature.

Nature, according to Mr. Baur, has three categories, defined as "the tangible world of land and water, the intangible world of light, sky and air, and the eternal forces of generation, growth and death which make up the cycles of life and season." The exhibition is accordingly divided into three sections, one for each of these aspects. The paintings displayed, however, seem uncomfortable in this impressive framework. As far as one can tell from the pictures themselves, only a few of the painters have subjects from nature, and those few are not really Abstract Expressionists. There is a Georgia O'Keeffe *From the Plains* with fat rumps of squatting storm clouds ready to thunder, a John Marin *Movement—Sea or Mountain, As You Will* with its play of mountain and valley, Karl Knath's somewhat thin Cubist reduction of a *Winter Wharf,* Lauren McIver's *Les Baux* and Joseph Stella's *Spring.* A few others present some suggestion of natural objects arrived at, perhaps accidentally, during the course of painting, like Charles Schucker's *The Tree* or Hans Moller's *Forsythias* (an action picture with yellow spots) or the handsome *Composition: The Storm* by Balcomb Greene which seems to me, with the possible exception of the Marin, the most successful and convincing picture in the show. But most of the works connect with nature only by their titles. Thus the Peterdi (neat rectangular draggings of a square brush dipped in blue paint), the Gorki (which looks like a congress of amorphous monsters), and the Frankenthaler (a large non-repeat pattern in colors suitable for a bedroom chintz) fit section one, The Land and the Waters, only in that they are respectively named *Tidal, Waterfall* and *Lorelei.*

In section two, Light, Sky and Air, nature is indicated by two more storms; a hastily painted *Red Sky* and a *High Snow—Low Sun,* both in the athletic brushwork style; a *Flight into Morning* and a *Golden Dawn,* exercises in pointillism without forms or images, a *Radiant Space* in primaries; a *Spring Twelve O'Clock* in interlocking rectangles like an architect's floor plan; a *Laureline* in grim black smears; and even a *Number 2.*

Cycles of Life and Season contains two *Februaries* (by different painters and four years apart), a *Drift of Summer,* a *Red Vine, Autumn, Dogtown,* and two other *Autumns* (both of '56 but one in Vermont), a *Black Dahlia,* a *Dead Leaves,* and a large vague, uncharacterized picture in shades of pink by Philip Guston with no name at all. However useful titles may have been for organizing the show, they bear little relation to the pictures themselves and seem more like names attached to identify the separate works than summations of what the pictures are about. At any rate, the part taken by nature to inspire the painter remains less than clear.

Nature, to a painter, is anything in the outside world he can touch or see. If he is to use nature as his subject he must clarify in visual terms the relation of this outside world to his inside self and attempt to describe this interplay to other people. Sometimes an abstract painter may take a motif from nature and generalize it into a comment on a particular style of painting or school of art. In this case he is using art history, not nature, as the subject of his work. Or he may attempt to arrive at some sort of general symbol for a class of natural phenomena.

Few of the painters presented in this exhibition try to do any of these things. Their subject matter appears to be for the most part a private emotion or an interior state. A subject matter as unspecific as this, however suitable for music, is difficult to communicate in visual terms. Most people simply fail to discover what the picture is about. Since the subject matter itself is unidentifiable, the painter is driven to find some striking idiosyncrasy of handwriting, to distinguish his pictures from others. This found, he has no need at all for subject matter. His talent can now be judged by the memorability of his formula, and his inspiration can be measured by the beauty of his paint and by the size of his canvas.

Why, then, all this fuss about nature? Few of these pictures are about it: few of the painters have been trained to confront it. Perhaps "nature" here is being given some new meaning. One is almost led to suspect from Mr. Baur's text that the word "nature" is being restyled against the day when "Abstract Expressionism" goes out.

The Museum of Contemporary Crafts is showing a beautifully presented selection of the works of Louis Comfort Tiffany. Tiffany was the most important and successful American decorator of the turn of the century working in the Medieval style. The style derived, as did pre-Raphaelite painting and Art Nouveau, from the Gothic revival of the early nineteenth century, and was distinguished by its insistence on handicraft—that is, handwork by artist-artisans—and by its modernization of the traditional grammar of ornament into contemporary and semi-realistic decorative forms.

Tiffany's stylistic framework, unlike that of William Morris and the earlier medievalists, was Romanesque rather than Gothic. His specialty was glass. His leaded glass windows were famous, the most extraordinary being a curtain made in 1911 for the stage of the National Theatre in Mexico City. He invented technical effects unknown to the Medieval tradition, the principle being an imitation of oil paint obtained by firing the glass with transparent colored glazes. But his greatest novelty was the use of translucent marbleized glass in a manner not unlike collage to supply modeling and to suggest natural textures. For folds in a drapery, clouds in a sky, or feathers in a wing, he would look for a piece of marbleized glass with a ripple pattern reproducing the modeling or texture he needed, and back it with colored glass to give the tint desired. The process was wasteful and very expensive. The results, if frequently harsh in design and vapid in sentiment, were always rich in color and varied in texture.

The present show has only one such window, an unimportant one without Tiffany's characteristic—and troublesome—late pre-Raphaelite iconography. His great skill and invention in the manipulation of glass is better shown in the small objects—vases, cups, plates, and tiles—done in what he called "Favrile glass." Their stylistic models are Roman, Saracenic, or Art Nouveau. Sometimes colored patterns are fused and blown into the fabric of the glass itself. Some have the surface iridescence of old Roman bottles. Everything has the pleasant irregularity of objects made by hand; everything is as different as possible from the functional forms and unified textures of present-day design. The colors and textures are rich and intricate; the shapes often more decorative and exotic than useful or beautiful. To us they seem pre-eminently period pieces. Their spindly flower forms, their butterfly-wing colors, and their Byzantine shapes and encrustations irresistibly call to mind some elaborate setting for Strauss's *Salomé*.

As in all the decorative work of the period, nature is constantly being mentioned—a window like a grape arbor, vases like flower calices, ten bronze lilies intertwined into an electric table lamp, or a lamp which is a bronze tree trunk with a leaded glass shade of branches, leaves, and fruit—a Tree of Knowledge for some library table. But just as in the Whitney show, nature is not the real subject of the work. Nor are the two exhibitions basically dissimilar. At the Whitney, the pictures' subject is private emotion, expressed by a spontaneous and unpremeditated use of paint. Here the subject is the evocation of a style, expressed by means of that greatest of all luxuries—handwork in a machine age. In each case color and texture are more interesting than content. And just as the medieval revival, of which Tiffany was a part, was a revolt in the art of decoration against the mechanical decoration and furniture of the industrial revolution, so in the same way this particular development of the Abstract movement can be regarded as a revolt—also perhaps in the art of decoration—against the dry, functional style of our own time.

# *Motion in Sculpture*

THE METROPOLITAN Museum is showing for the summer, in its somewhat forbidding gallery above the main entrance hall, a selection of French nineteenth and twentieth century sculpture—some seventy works of Degas, large bronze figures and small pieces by Rodin, female nudes by Maillol, a few Despiau portraits, a head by Brancusi entitled *Sleep,* and Bourdelle's well-known *Herakles.* Forty-five bronzes by Bourdelle were also on display at World House during June. The two exhibitions throw considerable light on the history of the sculpture of our time.

Rodin, the greatest of the nineteenth-century sculptors, derived from the Baroque tradition. In fact, some of the smaller bronzes and terra cottas might be mistaken for seventeenth-century Italian work. The distinguishing characteristic of this tradition is its preoccupation with form in movement. Its theory of modeling treated the human figure, its principal subject, as an articulated, moving skeleton over which rippled superimposed and interlocking waves of muscle and tendon. The surface of the statue was not to be arrived at by excavation into a block, by cutting away. It must be built up to, layer upon layer. The surface arrived at was in no way a static or final form. What was aimed at was the appearance of a temporary configuration of flesh and bone in movement from one position to another. These caught positions were not extremes of tension or relaxation; not the end points of a swing, but transition points along the flow of a continuous spiral. The spiral was held to be of such importance that it was sought for in all nature and in all movement. And even the movements of the stage and dance were planned as continuous progress along a spiral curve.

Thus Rodin's figures are neither in strain nor in repose. As far as I can remember, with one famous exception, they are all in motion: the *Man Walking,* caught in the motion of a step; *The Age of Bronze,* caught as if awakening from a dream. In his sculpture Degas has the same preoccupations. These bathing women and shying horses are painter's sketches not intended for display, studies of motion made as aids for painting.

Painters who work to any extent from memory have always used such sketches. The mind can remember a solid form better than one of its silhouettes. The particular outline a painter draws depends on the accident of where he stands in relation to his object, and the particular chiaroscuro he sees depends on how that object is lighted. But the solid form of the figure is relatively invariable, and it is much easier to remember the figure in the round and so to model it in clay, than it is to draw from memory one of its transitory appearances. When there are complicated problems of motion and chiaroscuro to deal with, painters have often made use of such three-dimensional models.

Because these figures are working sketches (and even more because of the extraordinary detachment of Degas' mind) they are more acceptable to us today than many of the Rodins, whose sentimental and emphatic sex appeal seems somehow dated. (Compare the woman in her circular bathtub washing her toes, or the thin little dancer with her foot advanced, her stockings wrinkled, waiting her cue, both in the Degas group, with the Rodin marbles, *Love and Psyche* or *The Hand of God,* whose soft, milky bodies, emerging from their beds of unworked marble, have irresistibly the air of candy figures on a wedding cake.) Nevertheless, both artists were following in a most serious and professional way the living tradition of sculpture of their time—the depiction of continuous, spiral motion.

With the advent of the twentieth century all this changed. Movement in sculpture seemed less interesting. It had become an academic formula. The static sculpture of Egypt and archaic Greece was adopted as the model to follow. Cézanne's dictum that all form can be analyzed into the simplicities of sphere, cylinder, cube, and cone became an undisputed working method. Sculptors were taught to obtain their modeling by cutting down to the form desired rather than by building up to it. The surface became smoother and more stylized. Streamlining—based on the motion of an unyielding body through a resisting medium—replaced the idea of a body moving by the interworking of its parts.

With Cubism even painting became static. And in the ballet the system of continuous movement was discarded—under, I believe, the leadership of Fokine—for the system, still used today, of instantaneous transitions from one static pose to another. One notices that photographs of contemporary ballet, taken as they are at the static end positions, are frequently more expressive than the dance itself.

Bourdelle's statue of Herakles drawing his bow, at the Metropolitan, is in one such static position, tense to move but not yet moving. His angry *Harlequin,* at the World House, is caught immobile, his staff back at the extreme end of its swing and at the point of beginning his blow.

Unlike the sculpture of Bourdelle, the Maillol girls have no movement at all. In a way they are the finest things the static school produced. By some wonderful, and perhaps French, sense of measure, they do nothing wrong. There are excesses neither of sex appeal nor of streamlining. The surfaces are still human. The results are nevertheless a little dull. Brancusi perfected a streamlining so elaborate and delicate that the variation of its surface can be detected only by the finger tips and his work becomes a sort of sculpture for the blind. With people of less talent, the static esthetic—elimination of movement and "cutting down" to the surface—and Maillol's influence toward sculptured figures with calves and ankles too heavy to move led to the decorative styles and tubular statuary of our century's international expositions.

This vulgarization of the static style we now find, at the mid-century, extremely tiresome, so it is not at all surprising that today the Lippold *Sun* in shimmering golden wire, and the Calder mobiles, where elegance is in lightness and where motion is an integral part of the the machine itself, enjoy enormous popularity. Even automobile design, which is acutely aware of current trends, has abandoned the streamlined teardrop for the much more entertaining image of the motor boat beating the waves. Motion in sculpture must be coming back.

# *American Genre Painters and the French Style*

THE NEWARK Museum is holding a summer show of the nineteenth century American painters in the genre style. Here boys are stealing watermelons, girls shelling peas, haymakers dancing, young men stealing kisses, people listening to war news, skating in Central Park, cooking maple syrup—exactly the kind of topical subject we find today treated meticulously on the cover of the *Saturday Evening Post* or sketchily on *The New Yorker*.

The works here made for domestic consumption—small household objects to add interest to a comfortable interior—are very like those which, for wider distribution, were published in lithographic copies by the firm of Currier and Ives. The style was hugely popular. There even existed in New York in the 1840's a Düsseldorf Gallery, named after the city which specialized in producing such anecdotal scenes.

Düsseldorf, not Munich, Rome, nor Paris, was where the painters went to study. Even those who did not go felt the influence of its school, which offered a practical method for painting these small and highly detailed works. The method was indirect: painting was done not after nature but after drawings the painter had made. With these for reference, he drew his picture with brown paint and then put on his colors. The shadows were thin—transparent and for the most part brown. Only the lights and the half-lights were colored. With thin shadows, a suitable varnish medium, and soft sable brushes, the work could be made as detailed as the painter desired or as the public for these pictures demanded.

We have certain prejudices today against the slick surface and the umber tonalities this method produces. But in the hands of a skillful workman the effects can be extremely handsome, particularly if the painter does not exaggerate his chiaroscuro. The side lighting of chiaroscuro with its accompanying heavy shadows, since here they are a uniform brown, will render the color unpleasantly heavy. One thinks of the amateur who said to Samuel Butler, "I know what color to paint the lights, but what color do I paint the shadows?" Here there is no question. Shadows are brown. The brown is there, not as a color or for color reasons. It is the necessary framework of the picture. At the same time it defines the tonality, harmonizes the colors, and permits quite wonderful dexterity in the painting of details.

A great many of the thirty-nine canvases shown—one for each artist—have chiefly an antiquarian interest. I myself would have preferred to see a larger representation of the vigorous men like William Sidney Mount, George Caleb Bingham and the young Winslow Homer. The picture by Mount, *Music Is Contagious, or Dance of the Haymakers,* is as skillfully done as any Messionier or Fortuny. The Bingham, a country contest—*Shooting for the Bull*—has a wonderful air of Poussin. The Richard Caton Woodville *War News from Mexico* is solid in drawing, handsome in color, and compact in composition. Enoch Wood Perry, Jr., is represented by a small canvas of admirable color and charming wit—a group of young men lounging on a hotel balcony in all the attitudes appropriate to a lazy Sunday afternoon. *Skating in Central Park* by the Hollander Johann Mongles Culverhouse has all the elaborate detail and aerial perspective of a seventeenth-century Dutch landscape.

The Metropolitan Museum has hanging for the summer some eighty French canvases, Modern and Impressionist, borrowed from private collections. A great many of these are already familiar in photograph and reproduction. It is nevertheless a great pleasure, and sometimes a great surprise, to see the pictures themselves. One could never have guessed from a reproduction the delicacy of color of Rousseau's *Carnival Evening*—all grays, browns, and blues—or the sophistication of its paint surface. This is not naïve painting. There is an unexpected Léger of a Southern French town, not in cubes at all, but with a hot blue sky over a hot hill-climbing street. The Gauguin *Still Life with Onions* has brilliant color put down in strands almost as if woven in tapestry. The Van Gogh self-portrait, belonging to Robert Lehman, to my surprise shows a receding chin, painted perhaps before the painter cultivated a beard. A Signac, of *St. Briac, Les Balises,* could be mistaken for the Seurats hanging next to it. I had not remembered the two painters were so much alike. Manet's *Mme. Brunet* is dressed in a black silk rep that only he could have painted. The sitter is touching and elegant, the painting luxurious and sober. Degas' beautiful *Chez La Modiste* shows the painter Mary Cassatt trying on a hat. Braque in *Under the Awning* gives the effect of blinding summer sunlight. The harlequin in Picasso's *Harlequin and Woman* has Picasso's face. But then Picasso has always put himself in his pictures; even the disturbing adolescent of his *Boy with Pipe,* now on show at the Museum of Modern Art, has some likeness to Picasso, based at least on a spiritual resemblance. Corot's *Bacchante and Leopard* is the handsomest of his figure pieces I have yet seen.

The striking thing about all these paintings, comparing them with the pictures in Newark, is the clearness of their tones and the immense variety of their color schemes. In this painting, color is never used as an added ornament on top of a design in monochrome. The color is a basic element of the picture. The painter begins his work with a brushload of colored paint. And each subsequent brush stroke is put down as a real color with a studied color relation to all the other colors on the canvas. The black-and-white value of the stroke defines the drawing of the forms he is constructing. But he never allows himself to forget that each brush stroke must be a patch of unambiguous color, no matter how small it may be. Even Corot, whose shadow framework is brown, never uses the same brown twice in a painting.

This is a Venetian tradition, brought to its perfection by the Tiepolos. In their works each tone of the modeling—light, middle tone, and dark—is a definite color. The warm-and-cold relationship of these tones is exaggerated. And the amazing brilliance these painters achieved with their relatively dull pigments comes uniquely from the careful harmony and contrast of these real tones.

This system of painting does not lend itself to the over-elaboration of detail. To make an unambiguous tone the paint must be put on fairly thick. Each color must be precise. Glazes and scumbles, which greatly facilitate detail, are enemies of frank tones. And with thick paint in definite color tones, tiny details are too unrewarding to be worth the trouble. Detail must be implied rather than stated.

As Max Jacob, who was also a painter, said, "It is inexactitude that saves us all."

Opaque paint in explicit color and no nonsense about what our ancestors called "finish"—that is the working method behind all these pictures. Nor was the question put to Butler at all inane. The answers to "what color to paint the shadows" would completely describe the methods of what we think of as the painting of our time.

# *The Drawing Styles*

THE GROUP of French drawings assembled from American collections for exhibit last year in Rotterdam and Paris has now returned to this country and is on view at the Metropolitan Museum. The collection is beautifully selected and comprehensive —more than two hundred examples chosen from the work of some eighty painters of the last four hundred years—from François Clouet's portrait of Francis II as a spoiled and suspicious boy of ten, done at the middle of the sixteenth century, down to a highly stylized version of a woman's face partly masked by two hands, apparently not her own, by Fernand Léger in 1952.

In the general high level of quality, certain names and works stick in the mind. Clouet's urbane and civilized faces, for example, contrast with the somber and meditative heads of François Quesnel, done two decades later and already so different in their interior life. The animation of Callot's little figures, the grace and style of Claude Lorrain (the beautiful drawing of two boats, and the one of an olive tree in a high wind), and the economy of the Watteaus are particularly memorable. There are topical scenes by Gabriel de Saint-Aubin and by Jean Michel Moreau (a comic ballet entrance at a party at court, and a visit of a foreign prince to a painting academy by Saint-Aubin; and by Moreau, a festival in honor of the Supreme Being in what is now the Champs de Mars). Prud'hon's nudes are embarrassingly sensual; Ingres' pencil portraits surgically immaculate. Daumier's raging irony embodies all the abuses of the law in the figure of one triumphant lawyer descending a courthouse stairs. The Seurats are uniform and mannered, the Picassos restlessly protean. Above all are the unforgettable drawings of Degas, particularly the sketch for a portrait of the painter Tissot, a most elegant young man sprawling at ease in the most elegant tailoring.

When we see so many at one time, we discover that painters' drawings come in three quite different kinds. First are the drawings made as ends in themselves or to be elaborated in some other graphic medium. Picasso's late drawings of Greek and mythological subjects, for example, fall into this category, as do the Daumier drawings made for newspaper publication; the Gravelots, which were studies for book illustrations; the Fragonards, intended to be engraved as a series of *estampes galantes;* and the Odilon Redons which appear to be sketches for lithographs or etchings. Drawings such as this, made to be shown and sold as drawing, or to be reproduced in one of the drawing-like processes, has great variety. It is highly individualized, since it aims to recall the painter's own work in oil, and closely reflects the stylistic mannerisms of its time.

The second kind of drawing has fewer graces. In this class are studies made to work out the composition of a picture. Such are the drawings by Poussin in which the figures are grouped as static blocks of sculpture all lighted from one side; the water-color drawings of Cézanne—studies in tensions of lines and masses later to be used in pictures; Claude's *Italian Seaport* with its planes of light and shadow brilliantly extemporized in hasty tones of ink; or Monet's one drawing at the Metropolitan show, a sketch for a *Déjeuner sur l'Herbe* where the figures and landscape are indicated only by the roughest penciling.

The third kind is drawings made from nature to be used, instead of nature, in finishing a picture. Here are the drawings by Clouet, Watteau, Degas, Corot, Ingres (made often as an end in themselves but always with the possibility of an oil in mind), de La Fresnaye's bandmaster and Picasso's young horseman, and mother and child. In these drawings made to paint from, individualized style is not important. The painter is interested only in preserving a clear and economical record of the visual facts before him. There is no need or time for added stylistic devices: these will develop automatically in the painting. So that all drawings made to paint from, whether by Clouet, or Degas, Pisanello, Watteau, or Pissarro, are alike in manner except for differences of hand and, except for differences of subject, bear little mark of place or epoch. And it is precisely this avoidance of style which gives the drawings made to paint from the grandest style of all—the style of unassuming mastery.

# *The German Expressionists*

THE MUSEUM OF MODERN ARTS is holding an exposition of German Art of the twentieth century—paintings, sculpture, and prints. The greater number of the painters shown are already well known in this country. Indeed, Kandinsky, Klee, and Ernst have major positions in the international hierarchy of the arts as ancestors and innovators. Franz Marc is remembered from the first appearance of modern art in this country for his cheerful primary colors, his stylized horses and his use of the Futurist fragmented and semi-transparent plane; and George Grosz, now a distinguished American painter, is popularly known as the bitterest satirist of the first postwar world. Kirchner, Beckmann, and Kokoschka have also achieved a wide renown. It is interesting to note that in the particular sampling given by this exposition, these internationally known painters are, on the whole, the ones most worth knowing.

The exposition starts with a North German group of the beginning of the century—with Paula Modersohn-Becker, Christian Rohlfs, and Emil Nolde. The two Modersohn-Beckers (a self-portrait holding a leaf and a peasant woman in an attitude of devotion) are heavy, wooden, and sentimental. The works of Rohlfs shown here, done in a fingerpainting style in brown and white, are too poor to offer an idea of what the painter's qualities might be. The Noldes are coarse in color, awkward in their thick paint, and vague and theatrical in drawing. His *Christ Among the Children* has the air—in a larger size—of a home-made Christmas card.

With Kirchner we are on other territory. He belonged to a Dresden group founded in 1905 which they called *"Die Brüke"* (The Bridge). Kirchner was a man of inquiring mind, open to French influence. His early picture of *Dodo and Her Brother* is a sensitive and entertaining characterization, almost a caricature, in the best Fauve style—the boldest possible brushwork and the brightest possible colors placed with the greatest possible knowledge of the effect they will produce. *The Street* (window shopping in a city), the *Market Place with Red Tower* and the *Artillerymen* (naked soldiers in a shower room being barked at by an officer) are done on a contemporary Parisian system—Cézanne screened through the Fauves, in particular through Delaunay. Kirschner's later pictures are executed in flat color areas in one of the current Post-Impressionist Paris styles. The other members of the "Bridge" group—Heckel, Schmidt-Rottluff, and Mueller—have cheerful color. But their insistent stylization of linear pattern reflects all that was least sympathetic in the painting of Montparnasse.

A later group called "The Blue Rider" included Marc and Kandinsky. Other members were Jawlensky and Macke; they were, if one can judge from the examples presented, the one a Berlitz Matisse and the other out of Renoir by some desiccated form of eclectic Cubism.

The canvases shown of Kokoschka I had not seen before except in reproduction. The portraits are sensitive; they might be called spiritualized in that they are pictures of the sitters' souls rather than of their bodies. The double portrait of Dr. Tietze and his wife is intimate almost to the point of mystical identification of painter and sitter; the portrait of Herwarth Walden is an intimate and not too sympathetic caricature. The painting, on the other hand, in both pictures is thin, unpleasant, put on in water-color washes, the canvas dirtied rather than covered, the color apparently out of the painter's control. The effect of the pictures is powerful; it is also unpleasant. The later landscapes, on the other hand, exemplified by the *London Bridge* in the present show, have enormous distance, air, richness, and variety of color, ease, spontaneity, charm, and conviction.

The group of painters who began showing in Germany after the First World War, represented in this show by George Grosz and Otto Dix, escaped or were deprived of the influence of the School of Paris. Their caricature is skillful and effective; their paint less so. Their paintings in oil as represented here are thin, precise, provincial, and competent. In Dix's portrait of *Dr. Meyer-Hermann*—the round, fat doctor in front of his round, fat X-ray machine—the unpleasantness of the painting may be taken as part of the joke. But in Grosz's portrait of the poet Hermann-Neisse, the equally mannered painting can serve no ulterior objective. Both Kurt Schwitters and Karl Hofer, who were older than Dix and Grosz, seem to have profited by France. Hofer's composition and drawing show the Cézanne influence, and his paint texture has the charm possessed by all the School of Paris. And Schwitters played with skill and Parisian grace the game of collage. On the other hand, their contemporary, Beckmann, in his genre pieces and allegories (*Family Picture,* the intellectual life in a garret; and *Temptation,* a triptych with on one side War and Mammon, on the other the Life of Luxury, and in the middle the Artist in Chains) has nothing of this. His line and composition seem to derive from Matisse rather than from any Cézanne influence. His painting is brutal and entertaining, with the harsh professional clarity of a high-style comic strip.

Painting from the Bauhaus is represented by works of Klee, Feininger, Schlemmer, and Kandinsky, all of whom taught there. The Klees shown here add nothing to what we already know. He remains a charming and fanciful painter with extraordinary invention in color and textures and a puckish wit. Feininger, on the other hand, has not aged well. The pictures now seem grimy and the Cubist grillwork, imposed on what is essentially representational landscape subject matter, appears dated and artificial. The Kandinskys of his Bauhaus period with their precise, thin, and labored patterns in vague and bodiless colors are much inferior to the richer, freer—and earlier—abstractions for which he is best known. Schlemmer's pictures once enjoyed a certain popularity. Now one sees stylized mannequins in modern-style interiors, and one wonders at their being shown at all.

The contemporary painting included in the show is in the neutral, non-objective manner found today in all officially sponsored international expositions.

It is almost certain that this is not the best display of German Expressionism that could be got together. After the First World War, when modern German painting first became available to the collector, it was, understandably enough, not very popular here, nor in France either. The best of it was distributed elsewhere or stayed at home. Just the same, whether on account of the choice of pictures or on account of the qualities of the painters themselves, I found myself, on the whole, disappointed. The prints and sculpture did not help. Everything seemed either an apocalypse or a caricature. Whatever painting skill there was seemed to have been learned in France. There is much that is impressive, much that is entertaining, much, even, to remember. But with few exceptions—a painting by Klee, a landscape by Kokoschka, a group of houses by Hofer—there is little to love.

# *Children's Painting*

THE GALERIE ST. ÉTIENNE is holding an exhibit of one hundred paintings by American school children on the subject of the Four Seasons. The Works on view have been chosen from among more than sixteen thousand entries. None of the painters is older than fourteen. The pictures have wonderful gaiety. The color is daring, vivid, and harmonious. In the work of a grown-up artist, their easy freedom and vivacity would denote unheard-of originality. Here, the spectator is pleased rather than astonished. Children's painting is a very special field and the rules that govern adult talent do not apply.

To the child artist the most important thing about his picture is its subject. No matter how abstract his picture seems to us, his principal interest was in telling a story. Otherwise he would have had no reason to paint it. Unlike the grown-up artist, he is little concerned with abstract beauty and not at all with depiction of visual space. The formal arrangement of his picture may be very good indeed. It is nevertheless not his primary concern; it is frequently the result of his unwillingness to waste any corner of his paper. The color we find so bold and beautiful is chiefly there to distinguish one object from another and to help him tell his story.

The space he depicts is motor, not visual—what he feels, not what his eye perceives. He draws things not as they appear to the eye but as they are found in the mind—as symbols, as ideas, as remembered feelings, or as numbers. He is careful to count—five fingers, two legs, one mouth. The table he draws lies flat so that it will be able to hold the Thanksgiving turkey. His men eating watermelon have circular mouths full of teeth and there are red drippings of watermelon juice. His lone ranger has a horse, a mask, a hat, a gun and a lariat. *Santa's Helper* is having huge fun with the impossible task of pushing a large fat Santa Claus headfirst down a very small chimney. In such pictures all the details are functional. Their undeniable charm was never part of the painter's conscious plan. The fascination is nevertheless there, the result, perhaps, of the fact that painting comes so easily for him.

A child's own sensations, his own motions, are more real to him than the things he moves among. He feels and lifts and touches rather than sees. These motor associations he has no trouble painting. In putting them down he has no need to struggle, as does the grown-up artist, with visual consistency or precise communication. He is his own audience, and works for his own pleasure.

But when he approaches adolescence, all this is changed. He is no longer the sole inhabitant of his universe. The visual aspect of the outside world becomes as real to him as his motor sensations of it. If he wishes to paint he must now communicate. His images must have some correspondence with what he sees and with what he now discovers other people see as well. He must fit these things into some sort of visual framework, some convention of perspective, some way of representing the more complicated universe he now inhabits. He adopts the tritest conventions of grown-up drawing—they are most like his own. He copies comic strips and pretty girls with lashes and cupid lips. Or, unable to cope with the newly revealed complexities of the visual world, he gives up in disgust. And his art teacher admits with sorrow that he has lost his talent.

It is possible that there is some way around this, some method of teaching drawing, some way of protecting the child from these too tempting vulgarities and too easy discouragements. It has not yet been found. There is no bridge between. And though a great many artists began to paint when they were still children, painting talent in a child is not a sign of adult talent to come, and the work of a mature painter has no relation whatsoever, either in kind or in skill, with what he might have done before the age of twelve.

Looking at this exposition, no one can deny that children's painting is a legitimate form of art. Here are paintings that would hold their own in any show: *Cotton Harvest,* for example, by Linda Cooler, age twelve, two children in a cotton field which whitens in the distance to an ominous sky and a row of sinister houses; *Hallowe'en Parade,* by Lilijean Miller, age nine, two sheeted figures carrying masks—which with its perfect placement and strange paint textures might have been by Klee; the funny *Skating and Falling* by Sharon Fye, age ten, with its beautiful use of gray and black with bright colors; *Winter Fun,* by John Kibler, age seven—a skating party all in blue; *Heat Wave,* by John Sarrechia, age thirteen, a panting tiger in a brown and red woods, as delicate as any Graves; and perhaps best of all, *Posing on the Beach* by Gladys Hoggard, age twelve—sunburned girls with beautifully excessive figures and wonderful hair-dos and bathing suits, as gaudy and elegant as Florine Stettheimer.

This is art and very good art, but there is something lacking. Unlike most art, it has intrinsic beauty, no intrinsic value. These paintings cannot be acquired; they have no prices. Nor are they—what we demand of painting today—a series of individual and irreplaceable productions. They are the flowering of an age group, not the expression of an artistic personality. They belong to the process of growth, not to the history of painting.

# *Amateur and Professional*

FORTY paintings by the world's most celebrated amateur, Sir Winston Churchill, are on view at the Metropolitan Museum. The subjects are still lifes, principally of flowers and landscapes painted on sunny days. The painting method is a basic

Impressionism. The painter works from nature, putting down on his canvas with as little rearrangement as possible the flat shapes of the colors he finds in the subject before him, his eye half closed to eliminate detail. He allows himself only the liberty of exaggerating the color intensity of the more neutral tones, of rendering brown by a richer orange or lavender for gray.

Judged by amateur standards, Churchill's work is extraordinarily good. His colors are clean and gay like good English decoration. And several of the canvases are so completely lacking in technical faults that, in the absence of the other pictures, they might well be mistaken for the work of a professional—which is highest possible praise for the talented amateur.

The amateur painter is a great deal more concerned than the professional with the problem of giving his work a professional appearance. He lacks professional training and his painting is likely to be disfigured by faults of drawing, tone relation, and composition which the professional painter has early learned to avoid. But even when these faults are absent, the amateur's painting can always be distinguished from the professional's by a quality shared by all amateur work—the complete absence of original ideas.

The amateur painter is in general a cultivated man who has discovered the pleasures of painting and pursues it as recreation and sport. The approach he adopts may be a form of Impressionism, or even of Abstraction, depending on his age group and education, but it will necessarily be a thoroughly familiar one. He is interested in playing a fascinating game, not in making up new rules. He is visiting a world already explored by other painters rather than creating and imposing a world of his own. His real originality has already found its expression elsewhere. Otherwise he would long ago have quit his own profession for that of painter, as Gauguin gave up a career on the stock exchange in his pursuit of art. The price of originality is undivided love.

The naïve painter, like the amateur, is also characterized by lack of originality, but in quite a different way. The amateur painter is in general a member of the educated classes, familiar with painting.

Consequently, he has available to him for the expression of his ideas, however commonplace they may be, a great variety of possible painting styles. Naïve painting, on the other hand, embodies the pictorial concepts of the uneducated, which may be very original indeed. Where the naïve painter lacks originality is in style. He has not been taught to draw, to break up the visual world into its elements of line, shape, form, color, and perspective. He does not paint what he sees; he paints what he knows is there, a conceptual world composed of verbal symbols, where walls have bricks, where trees are green and have denumerable leaves, where faces are composed of eyes, ears, a nose, a mouth, and hair. These symbols are the material out of which all naïve painting is made. Consequently, all naïve pictures, in spite of the fresh and charming ideas they frequently contain, are surprisingly alike, even to color and scale. The naïve and amateur painters also have this in common, that the ones who have gained the public's attention owe it more to accident of publicity and caprice of collector than to their technical interest in the profession itself.

Painting such as this may have no place in the history of art. It nevertheless provides immense pleasure and instruction to the people who do it. And I, as a professional painter, view with much more sympathy the amateur, seated before his "motif," happily and quietly communing with nature in water color, than I can feel for the ubiquitous amateur photographer with his gadget bag and meters, nervously preparing to perform on nature an impersonal and surreptitious extraction. The painter is the more civilized man.

Peter Blume, known for his large, detailed, semi-allegorical pictures, is showing at Durlacher's two important finished pictures along with the drawings and sketches used in their making, as well as some thirty independent drawings in pen-and-ink—the whole done during his recent residence at the American Academy in Rome. The drawings, in a firm linear style with a broad-nosed pen, could not be handsomer. The hand is accurate, the execution astonishingly free and convincing. The drawings and sketches leading up to the paintings are also very fine. The finished paintings, however, have little of the drawings' quality.

The themes of the pictures are intricate and promising. The smaller—*Hadrian's Villa*—depicts an olive harvest, the tree in center, its branches filled with men with poles, its roots covered by a circle of cloth to collect the falling olives. The more ambitious—*Passage to Etna*—presents a shorthand history of Rome: from the bottom of the canvas a pyramid of drums and capitals of antique columns rises into the uncovered crypt of a catacomb, in the recesses of whose walls human skeletons lie exposed, while above this is an open street of tenements with festoons of laundry and crowds of small people with sad, sallow faces.

The drawings and plans for both pictures are full of dash and bravura. In the finished work all this is lost. The painting is labored and heavy. The broad circular movement of the composition, so handsome in the sketches, is obscured. The color is bright but inexpressive. There is no light and no real air. And in spite of the sad story told by the sad faces—absent in the sketches and serving here apparently to demonstrate the artist's social consciousness—the work succeeds in being only quaint and puckish, like illustrations for some fairy tale for children. Comparing the pictures with the drawings for them, it is obvious that something unfortunate has intervened between the conception and the finished product. The difficulty, I suspect, is an excess of professionalism. For if the excellence of an amateur painter can be seen in how well he comes up to professional standards, the excellence of the professional can be judged by how well he avoids them.

By professionalism, I mean too great a respect for professional standards. The painter wishes above all to demonstrate his professional competence. In this aim he tries to prove too many things, to show himself capable of solving all problems in one picture. He works too hard, is too scrupulous, tries to please too many people, loses his idea and ends by exchanging spontaneity for decorum. It would be a great pity if so fine a talent as Peter Blume's were to stay caught in such a tiresome trap. He should know by now that competence has nothing to do with professional conformity. Competence makes its own standards. Because, as Juan Gris once said, one becomes a classic by not resembling the classics at all.

# *Form and Content*

THE WORK of the French painter Edouard Pignon is now being shown at the Perls Gallery. The pictures are principally landscapes, views of the Mediterranean countryside—hills with houses, trees, and vineyards—subjects such as Cézanne or Derain might have painted, done in the bright, clear colors of Matisse. The novelty of the pictures is that this basic material is manipulated so that at first sight it could be mistaken for the free Abstractions of Kandinsky.

Such superimposition is characteristic of our time. Picasso and Stravinsky are full of it—one subject matter dressed up in another's style: Cézanne's harlequin seen in the guise of a New York skyscraper or a jazz concerto fitted out as an opulent parody of late baroque. But unless the artist's invention and the vitality of his subject dominate his stylistic references, the work will be brilliant rather than original, and will soon wear thin.

Pignon is a gifted painter. In certain of the pictures, as in *La Colline de Bandol,* with its carefully planned architecture of railroad-cutting, field, and hill, the combination of natural view and imposed pattern works extremely well. In others, the color is more decorative than functional, and the design wiggles as restlessly as any Arthur Rackham. In all, the work has something of the splashy virtuosity of a travel folder. One thinks of a commercial artist, more interested in his own skill than by the imposed commonplaces he is hired to illustrate. It is the old problem again, of form and content, a problem that is particularly vexing in our time.

Two other expositions now current offer extreme and opposite examples of this. One is the show of Charles Schucker at the Passedoit Gallery. The work is a form of drip painting. White pigment, poured like thick cream onto a heavy, unprimed, cotton sail-cloth, forms the compositional framework of the composition—a ribbon-like handwriting subsequently tinted by dilute washes of strong color which spread and settle in the interstices of the canvas. The shapes thus defined evoke landscapes and posturing human figures. Their fluid grace and muted expressivity bring to mind a faded estheticism of another time, some minor follower of the pre-Raphaelites. The textures are refined and ingenious, the color combinations limited, the total effect monotonous and trivial.

The work of Charles White, shown a few doors away at the ACA Gallery, is in every way Schucker's exact opposite. The pictures are large drawings, principally in chalk with pen-and-ink on very large sheets of paper. The subjects are Negro men and women, life size, in heavy sculptural modeling. The background is either a vague fog or a detailed backdrop with little relation to the figures. Composition is perfunctory. Everything has been sacrificed to the human warmth of gesture and feature. The isolation of the figures from the background, their oversize, the rounded drawing of the forms, altogether produce an intense emotional projection, comparable only to the crayon enlargements of family photographs one used to find in small country farm houses.

Schucker and White, each in his own way, are extremely skillful. If they are interesting, however, it is because they present instructive and extreme examples of what professional painters have always known that painting should not be. The one illustrates shape without content; the other, content without form.

A heresy is an exaggerated truth. The heresy exemplified by

Charles Schucker is that painting is only a craft; that pictures are made not by the development of images, but by the manipulation of materials. The painter's attention is on design—on color and texture—and he is little concerned with the particular image the work evokes. Though any smudge or wiggly line inevitably engenders pictorial associations, these associations, supplied by the subconscious mind, are an unimportant adjunct. The picture is to be judged not by the emotional appeal of its images, but by the memorability of its design, the individuality of its paint, and the elegance of its calligraphy. This is the approach to painting that is most generally taught in art schools today where the systematic neglect of all purposeful communication limits painting to decoration and places it squarely among the applied arts.

The work of Charles White directed uniquely to the illustration of human sentiment exemplifies the opposite heresy, a heresy that is the extreme result of the painter's training as it was formerly understood. The painter has learned to draw and nothing else. He has been taught little about color, scale, paint handling, or composition. He knows only how to represent on a flat surface the solid forms he sees and feels in nature. These forms have intense emotional connotations. But how to transpose and confine them to a canvas, to make them into a picture, he has not learned. Nor has he learned, as Cézanne did, that painting is not sculpture. So that he will sometimes even try to paint by putting transparent colors on top of a drawing in black and white as one would tint a photograph. Just the same, such work, in spite of its lack of pictorial amenities, is likely to have a great popular appeal on account of the direct and unveiled emotional force possessed by any convincing representation of the human form.

Both these approaches to painting are equally unacceptable. One is elegant and esoteric, the other warm and intimate. Both are easily perverted. The elegance of form without content lends itself all too quickly to industrial layout and packaging, while unhampered emotion, sentiment without art, leads straight to the inanities of soap opera and to the terrifying generalities of propaganda.

# *The Artist Abroad*

UNDER the title *A Change of Sky,* the American Academy of Arts and Letters is showing—along with a similar literary exhibition—some seventy-five American pictures chosen for having been painted abroad. The works range in time and kind from a sentimental *Savoyard Boy,* done in The Hague by Eastman Johnson in 1853, to an Abstract *Forms on a Table* by Patrick Henry Bruce, painted in Paris in 1930 in the primary-colored Dutch-style Cubism so fashionable there that year.

As is normal enough in any exposition with a set theme, the quality of the pictures varies enormously. On the credit side, there is one of the best of the Mary Cassatts, on loan from Boston; a charming Maurice Stern of 1903 of ladies and merrymakers on *Bastille Day in Paris,* without any of Stern's later linear hardness; fine landscapes by Twachtman, Charles A. Platt, and Inness; some masterful Duvenecks; an unexpectedly excellent Eilshemius from Samoa; two brilliantly colored Haitian scenes by Gifford Beal; an even more brilliant Cubist still life by Alfred Maurer; the least conventionalized Arthur B. Davies I have seen—a wide-angle landscape of Italian hill-town and valley; an enchanting John La Farge of lagoon and palm-covered atoll with wading fisherman; and a beautiful water color by Maurice Prendergast of the Piazza San Marco, with flags, in a representational style quite different from the work of his I know. On the debit side are several of the less interesting early Winslow Homer English seacoast water colors; a painted, gilded, and incised decorative gesso panel by Charles (not Maurice) Prendergast, quite without quality; a vulgar, if entertaining, Elihu Vedder of Roman maidens in pre-Raphaelite Greek draperies, bathing and cavorting on a strand; and an equally vulgar but just as diverting work by Robert F. Blum—a Japanese street scene with candy vendor and children, painted in picayune detail and framed in a filigree of gold lacework—the show's one example of the 1880 French salon style.

As this array of pictures painted abroad serves to demonstrate, there are two distinct reasons why painters travel: Either they go to Europe as students, to learn the trade; or, as mature artists, they travel the world in search of the picturesque. The first reason is the more decisive. The early training a painter receives determines both his stylistic advantages and the level of his professional competence. Perhaps the most revealing thing to know about any painter is where he went to school.

Take Duveneck for an example. His training in a Munich that specialized in old-master technique (of glazes, varnish medium, with rich, brown, transparent shadows on a tinted ground) forever formed his painting manner. Inness' work as a young man in the school of Daubigny was responsible for his pre-Impressionist, atmospheric style. Whistler's Japanese and Manet influences were acquired in his student days in France where also, as young people, Theodore Robinson and Mary Cassatt became real Impressionists and Alfred Maurer a real Cubist. And Marsden Hartley's bright tones and massive brushwork stem directly from the Fauvism and Expressionism he encountered as a young man in France and Germany. Whereas Elihu Vedder would probably not have undertaken his high literary allegories, nor would he have executed them in so stringy and linear a style, had he not studied in Italy—in his day, as far as painting went, the most provincial of the major European countries.

Traveling for subject matter has much less influence on the painter. When John La Farge went to Samoa, it was for subject matter alone. He was already a formed painter with a watercolor manner acquired at home by making sketches for stained glass windows. But this training was provincial and insufficient. And despite his pictures' extraordinary charm, they are sadly lacking in professional quality, and the one oil on display here is quite inept. Maurice Stern went for exotic subject matter to Bali, Italy, and elsewhere. But being Paris-trained, he painted it all in the characteristic manner of the Cézanne-influenced École de Paris of the twenties. In the same way, Guy Pène du Bois went to paint in France. But the mannerisms of figure drawing in his pictures here shown demonstrate that the painter was really New York-trained. His ball-headed and cylinder-bodied personages derive from a literal interpretation of Cézanne's dictum that all forms can be analyzed into combinations of cylinders, cube, and sphere—a limited view which formed the basis of a mannerism much in favor in New York when Du Bois was a student.

Perhaps it matters less today where a painter goes to school, since everywhere in the world the student has available to him identical instruction in modern art. And though the style originated in Paris some fifty years ago, it is in schools away from Paris that its basic patterns are now most efficiently taught. Just the same, as the pictures in this exposition illustrate, there is a fundamental difference between the professional traditions handed down in the great painting centers, and the rather narrow range of mannerisms taught and cherished elsewhere. If I were a young painter intent on learning my trade, I would prefer to study it where the most pictures were being made and sold and where the greatest variety of techniques and traditions was available—in Paris, or in New York perhaps, but not in Rome or Venice or Ann Arbor.

# MARKET REPORTS

# *Picasso's Ceramics*

MORE THAN a hundred ceramics by Picasso are on display at the Cooper Union Museum. It is the largest group yet to be seen in New York—vases, decorative plaques, bowls, and pitchers, by the liveliest painter of our time.

The work comes in three kinds. First there are the unique examples, modeled or designed by Picasso himself and glazed and decorated by his hand. Others, stamped *Empreinte Original de Picasso* and existing in some hundred copies, are pressings in unglazed white biscuit or red clay from molds made by the painter. A few, marked *Edition Picasso,* are factory copies or interpretations of Picasso originals and, as far as I can see, in no way inferior. These pressings and editions, made at the Poterie Madura in Vallauris under Picasso's supervision, are popular with collectors. Their price cannot be prohibitive.

The work is cheerful and witty. The shapes vary from parodies of standard ceramic models to the most bizarre improvisations. The surface ornamentation is done with an easy, flowing hand and unfailing invention. There are vases adorned with a nude model and her bearded painter, plates with faces and street scenes, a pitcher in the form of a fighting cock, the lines of its decoration forming at the same time the bird's plumage and a grotesque mask, a pitcher in the shape of a pigeon with its tail in air, another like a duck clasped by two hands. There are bulls and bullfighting, classical figures, goats, owls and flowers, and many fish. The pieces are all handsome and reassuringly unfunctional; it might be difficult to eat from some of the plates or lift some of the pitchers. They are designed as art objects, made to fit contemporary decoration.

In this country two styles of interior decoration are ordinarily available—modern and period. The one imitates the functional efficiency and shiny neatness of new machinery. The other uses antiques to evoke the past or aims at a harmony composed of disparate styles. There also exists a third style of decoration—called in France *le style auberge*—the style of the country inn. It uses country materials—provincial or peasant furniture, dark woodwork, plaster walls, pewter pots, regional earthenware, handwoven rugs and hangings, and, in its more popular versions, red-checked tablecloths and cart wheels made into chandeliers. A version of it was prevalent here some forty years ago under the name of "mission," and still exists in a more elaborate form in Frank Lloyd Wright interiors and in seemingly endless variations in the do-it-yourself designs of the household magazines.

It is in this peasant style of decoration that the ceramics of Picasso, unlike his paintings, are so beautifully at home. They have not the delicacy of design and elaboration of drawing we are accustomed to find in period pieces, and nothing of the machine-like asepsis and humorless severity of the modern style. Part of the work's charm is that it is, technically speaking, crude. Picasso is not willingly expert in the troublesome chemistry of clay and glazes. As he himself says: "I do not search; I find." But the lovely good humor and impish vitality of the pieces make them appear less like work of the grand old man of painting than like the playful and charming creations of some prodigious child.

# *Nadelman, Maurer, and Dali*

ELIE NADELMAN'S figurines, on show at the Hewett Gallery, are an attempt to solve the contemporary sculptor's most serious problem—how sculpture is to survive without a market. For sculptors, recent times have been uncompromisingly hard. The human figure, sculpture's consecrated subject which even the most prudish Victorians considered a necessary adornment for public buildings, has become too risky, costly, and ornate for the economical style of our contemporary architecture, and sculptor's commissions have become extremely rare. Nadelman sought another market, a domestic one, by publishing his works, like books or records, in large editions. Copies of paintings made by the systems of reproduction in use today are not good, as one can see by comparing any color print with its original. Sculpture, on the other hand, is for the most part cast from a mold. It is already, in its natural state, a sort of replica. And if one wishes to multiply the process, the succeeding copies are also replicas with every virtue of the original. Thus Nadelman hoped to convert the art of figurative sculpture to domestic uses, now that there is no longer a demand for large public pieces, by turning out these small figures in multiple examples and inexpensive materials.

The idea was not new nor do I think it has proved very fruitful. But the stuff itself is extraordinarily handsome—single female figures and groups, five to nineteen inches high, in papier-mâché and terra cotta, painted and unpainted, glazed and unglazed. The figures themselves have something of the heavy-bodied, quasi-cylindrical style one finds in so much of the 1920 work, from Maillol, Lachaise, and Manship, from Picasso's "Classical" nudes and the painting of Bellows and Guy Pène du Bois, on to the style's unfortunate apotheosis in the Paris 1925 *Exposition des Arts Decoratifs*. But the small scale of Nadelman's pieces and the boldness and delicacy of their veiled modeling remove the doctrinaire heaviness inherent in this classic revival style. One is inescapably reminded of the figurines of Tanagra which, apart from their extraordinary grace, these figures resemble not at all.

On seeing the Alfred Maurer retrospective at the Bertha Schaefer Gallery, one cannot help comparing it with the retrospective recently held at the Downtown Gallery of the figure painting of Max Weber. Both painters, as young men in Paris, enthusiastically joined forces with the revolutionaries of modern art. Weber was the more determinedly modern: if one relates the dates of the pictures in his recent show to the various styles in which they were painted, one discovers that in this sequence of Parisian fashions, Weber was consistently in step. Beginning with a nude of 1907 in a manner then practiced by Suzanne Valadon, the painter seems to have passed through the influence of Cézanne (in a handsome life-class study in orange and green) to discover in 1910 Picasso's African Negro style; then on in 1913 through a form of Futurism to arrive in 1917 (the two best pictures of the show) at the bright-colored Cubism with spots of Picasso's ballet *Parade;* on in 1932 to Picasso's "Neo-Classical" heavy figure manner; and finally, in 1945, to something that looks strangely like the wiggly line of Archile Gorky. Apart from the painter's topical versatility, the most extraordinary thing about this sequence is the way in which he has managed to impose on each successive manner his own trademark in the form of a stereotype caricature of the Jewish face.

Maurer's retrospective has less variety. Starting with a portrait of a woman in kimono of about 1901, in subdued tonalities and Japanese space division that show Whistler's influence, he passed around 1908 through a brilliant Fauve period with the most beautiful and gaudy colors, to arrive in the mid-twenties at the analytical Cubism he never thereafter abandoned—a style in which the lines and planes of the objects painted, generalized and extended, form the network that is the picture's composition. The colors are varied, the line simplified but not in the least mechanical. The work, like Weber's, reflects the most advanced in European art. Both men were caught, bedazzled by the new techniques, like Indians at the coming of the white man. But where Weber, disoriented, stayed on the side lines and pilfered, Maurer understood, assimilated, and joined. His work may be not as brilliant or as talented as Weber's but its elements seem more digested and their expression more natural and sincere. And the best of it—like his elongated self-portrait in a soft hat, and his Cubist synthesis of Gilbert Stuart's *Washington*—is difficult to forget.

Salvador Dali is holding at Carstairs his most entertaining exhibition here in many years. Dali has always been a master of the gag:

witness the works by which one knows him best, his depictions of the unruly world of dreams painted in a serene and decorous pre-Impressionist style. A similar marriage of incongruities dominates the present exhibition. Here references to the *Sistine Madonna* and to Velasquez' celebrated *Infanta* replace the Freudian imagery of his earlier work, and this homage to Renaissance painting is for the most part executed in zigzag brush strokes claimed to describe the path of atomic particles in a cloud chamber—a wonderful amalgamation of photographic realism, abstract calligraphy, and popular nuclear physics. The largest picture in the show has an even more extraordinary triple-take. From close up it appears completely non-objective—a uniform diagonal grillwork of white and black circles on a background of gray bespangled with splinterlike brush strokes in pink. From halfway across the room the pattern of strokes becomes a Madonna figure, while from still greater distance the black and white circles are seen to be a huge magnification of the dots in a halftone print representing an enormous ear (the catalogue says an angel's).

Dali has always been an excellent miniaturist. Even this biggest picture derives part of its quality from its resemblance to a minute image mechanically enlarged, and among the other canvases the small ones are the best. The mixture of calligraphic brushwork with meticulous representation is most convincing when the scale is small; in certain of the larger pictures the smoothly painted passages of flesh retain something of the oil-cloth quality so unpleasant in his devotional pictures of recent years.

These works, presumably designed in conformity with Catholic dogma, nevertheless show evidence of commercialism deeply distressing in so vigorous an artist. The distinguishing marks of commercialism are these: a humorless and respectful treatment of conventional subject matter; a style of execution adapted from familiar masterpieces of established value; and most inescapable of all, an overworked and insensitive surface texture. These marks have all been visible in Dali's recent paintings. And it is a pleasure to find in the present exhibition less of such commercialized surfacing and some of the playful and technically unconstrained inventiveness of his earlier years.

# *Bratby and Wyeth*

ONE OF the most entertaining shows of the early winter—John Bratby at French and Company—consisted of fourteen large paintings on board, some five of which were commissioned for the movie version of Joyce Cary's novel *The Horse's Mouth* to represent the work of Gulley Jimpson, its painter hero. A painter myself and interested in such things, I have twice tried to read the book and twice given it up. Jimpson is not a painter; he is a literary man's idea of what a painter is like. He thinks in color words, loses his painting kit, has no working habits and leaves his brushes dirty. A painter in his off-hours may lead an irregular life, but he is usually methodical in his work.

Bratby is a great deal better than this, quite good enough to express in paint the violence of Jimpson's romanticized character. His pictures are ugly, brilliant, vulgar, and skillful. They could be copied in mosaic without change. There is no chiaroscuro. Lines and dots of bright, thick color—like the irregular bits of colored glass in mosaic—serve to define the modeling. The compositions are casual and crowded. The subject matter is English artistic life in lower middle-class surroundings, presented without graces or amenities: full-length multiple portraits of brutally unattractive people, and interiors with doors, wallpaper, children, toys, books, television sets, and the other concomitants of urban living. Frequently the hands and feet of the artist painting are included—a perhaps unnecessarily discordant signature. Skillful and willfully shocking, much of the work's violence derives from an intentional confusion of categories—from painting a domestic subject in a mural style.

Andrew Wyeth recently closed at Knoedler's the most talked-about exposition of the season, inasmuch as one of his pictures sold for $35,000—an unheard-of price for a young contemporary. The water colors are unexceptionally beautiful, the best in the Winslow Homer tradition I have yet seen: New England sea and countryside subjects, restrained and subtle in color, easy and exact in execution. The pictures on canvas seemed less good. They are done, I am told, very slowly, not more than three works a year, and in some form of tempera emulsion—a medium which lends itself better to elaboration than to breadth. The drawing is often labored, the detail overscrupulous, the color dead. In spite of the harsh and elegant oddity of their pictorial ideas and compositions, the pictures are difficult to remember. It is as though the vigor of the painter's concepts could not quite survive the labors of execution. For a meticulous temperament, emulsion paint can be a dangerous tool.

# *The Ash Can School—Victor Brauner, Stephen Greene, and Benjamin Kopman*

THE FIFTIETH anniversary of the first group exposition of the eight painters known as the "Ash Can School" falls this month, and the Hirschl and Adler Gallery is holding through February a memorial exhibit of some fifty canvases of Robert Henri, affectionately remembered as the most facile and charming of the eight. Henri was a virtuoso, working directly on his canvas without previous preparation or subsequent retouching, his brush loaded with paint and freely lubricated with oil. The tradition is an old and respectable one, going back to Hals and Magnasco and practiced by painters as different in point of view as Boldini and Manet. But here in the figure pieces by which Henri is best known—the Gipsy singers and models, the smiling children—this virtuoso tradition seems to have reached its ebb. The drawing is hasty, the edges hard, the color unconsidered, either muddy or too clean, the scale overlarge. Every easy effect has been exploited: mouths are full of teeth and laughter, eyes gleam with highlights. The pictures were obviously painted for exhibition. They have aged quite badly.

On the other hand the tiny sketches, some no larger than three inches by five, are a surprise and a delight—the Luxembourg Gardens, the banks of the Seine, the Bal Bullier, strollers in the Maine woods. The paint is fresh, the composition free, the color inventive, the values exact, and all with a busy and careless charm not unlike the painting of Vuillard. Here the painter's virtuosity is properly employed and the pictures are not unworthy of the late Impressionist tradition from which they spring.

As part of this anniversary, James Graham and Sons are showing two other members of the eight—Everett Shinn and Arthur B. Davies. Davies is represented by a group of his characteristic nudes and by a few landscapes. The work is stylized, gentle, decorative. The water colors and pastels are more successful than the oils which, with their thin washes of bright colors, seem more like prints than paint. The patterned groupings of nudes, asexual, elongated and unreal, and the wallpaper-like landscapes, vaguely reminiscent of the English fan painter, Charles Conder, are skillfully done and probably at some later date will recapture our interest. Today the sources of their mannerisms are too apparent, their connection with the fashion drawing of the '20s all too clear. Their milky charm seems singularly out of place in our ruder world.

Everett Shinn is a much more vigorous painter, with something of the facility of a popular illustrator. As with Davies, his oils are on the whole less interesting than his pastels and water colors. His principal subject is New York—stage and street scenes, many of them done at night—and he treats it with love, amusement, and respect. The scale is elegant and small. The drawing could not be more skillful or the representation of light more convincing. There are no false effects, no modish references to fashionable art. Even his debt to Degas is less than one had thought. His work stands by itself—a worthy tribute to a magnificent city.

Victor Brauner, shown at Iolas, is accurately described in his catalogue as a painter-poet. He is one of a group of painters and poets who called themselves Surrealists and whose aim, more literary than pictorial, was to introduce the unconscious into art. For this they employed all manner of psychological disciplines, from word association games and dream interpretation to artificially induced paranoiac states and the techniques of black magic.

Brauner's pictures present themselves as elaborate symbolic diagrams. Their style derives in part from American Indian drawings and Navajo sand paintings—flat, linear men and animals, schematized as if for weaving in a rug. Another series depicts these personages drawn as if constructed of folded and intersecting cutouts of colored cartridge paper. Their precise meanings I am too little versed in Surrealism to explain. It is probably partly systematic—based on alchemical and magical symbols—and partly hermetic and personal. The titles, with their characteristic Surrealist puns, are amusing and sometimes even revealing—as in the two small pictures *Victor* (the painter's name) *Semivictorescent,* a crescent moon with limbs, and *Victor Victorescent,* a full moon or sun; *Poisson d'Honneur* whose title, and perhaps subject, seems to derive from the telescoping of *poisson d'avril* (April fool) with *vin d'honneur* (formal reception); or *l'Illustre Mamalogue,* a figure with breasts; or the schematic layout describing *le Poet en Exile.* The pictures themselves are gay and handsome, their primitivism convincing, and their mysterious iconography extremely titillating, particularly as they present an aspect of Surrealism quite different from the more familiar images of Ernst, Dali, or Tanguy.

New pictures by Stephen Greene are being shown at Grace Borgenicht's. The work is more Abstract than before. The personages, with their round heads and bellies and rachitic limbs, reminiscent of the figures of the Italian sculptor Marino Marini, are still present but now more difficult to make out. The color is brilliant and beautiful: oppositions of warms and colds, sometimes at their highest intensity—clear blues set against rich reds and oranges —sometimes in paler pastel shades. The subject matter, according to the titles and to the preface to the catalogue, is deeply tragic. There is a *Cain and Abel,* a *Prophesy,* a *Nemesis,* a *Flagellation.* The canvases themselves, with their dry, fresco-like surfaces and clean colors, seem pleasantly gay, somewhat reminiscent of the buxom and modestly official work of Maurice Denis, the French mural painter of the twenties.

Another painter with a tragic subject matter, Benjamin Kopman, is being shown by World House. Kopman paints landscapes and old people. The style, which could be called either brutal or powerful, belongs to the near-caricature tradition of Rouault, Gropper, or Forain. The drawing is rough and solid. The paint application is heavy, not unlike that of the young Cézanne. The color is extremely beautiful, rich, deep, and sober. The landscapes are finer than the figure pieces, whose lumpy forms and insistent caricature seem to me both insensitive and over-violent. The painting has no intellectual pretensions whatsoever, but it is warm and harshly human.

Both Greene and Kopman take as their subject human infirmity, and Greene's catalogue in particular is at some pains to stress his preoccupation with the theme:

> In Greene's pictures the victim and the victor, the tortured and the torturer, in the face of irreconcilable demonic powers by which they are possessed, are united in a compassionate bond. . . .

The next sentence seems less clear:

> Greene's formal development has been toward a style in which colors and shapes, rather than signifying the emotions expressed through this subject, would themselves, as it were, be permeated by them. . . .

Apparently the shapes and color do not express emotions; they feel them.

> He has arrived at this stage because of his search to paint in a manner in which the symbolic potency of his imagery would be contained and retained within the formal world of the picture with a maximum staying power.

In other words, the pictures are a good, solid investment.

Kopman's preface is a great deal simpler:

> Well here I am; in everybody's judgment (except perhaps my own) I am an old man. And yet I am devoting myself to that primal emotion which was kindled in me in my youth, the love of the world, for people and trees, for the sky and the earth, dreaming of these now as in my distant past, and paying tribute to God and his important creations with words and images.
>
> Because we live in an age of speed some people who never cared for art turned away from my work using the excuse that it has not moved fast enough. They do not realize that the very speed they so admire now will fly them by, and they

will remain wondering what has happened. In my seventieth year I am most grateful to fate that it has endowed me with patience and a sense for timelessness.

# *Magic Realism*

SOME THIRTY or more works of Raphaelle Peale—still lifes, "deceptions," and miniatures—done in the first quarter of the last century, are on show at Knoedler. Raphaelle was the eldest son of Charles Willson Peale, the well-known Philadelphia artist who, in his passionate devotion to the art, named most of his children after painters. There were Angelica Kauffman Peale, Rembrandt Peale, Rubens, Titian, Sophornisba Anguiciola, and Rosalba Carriera Peale. Several even took up the profession. Raphaelle himself had little success in it. He seems to have been lively, unfortunate, and somewhat dissipated, a good mimic and ventriloquist, and never very prosperous. The miniatures on view are skillful and evidently very resembling. "His price is ten dollars" runs one of his advertisements. "No likeness, no pay." The still lifes which form the major portion of the show are compactly composed and carefully painted, small and neat, like Dutch seventeenth-century work but with none of the Dutch opulence.

The "deceptions"—paintings of cards and scraps of paper pinned to a board—are microscopic in rendering. Even the news print is legible. The most engaging of the pieces, the "covered picture" called *After the Bath,* is a joke, a picture of a picture. It is a representation in *trompe l'oeil* of a painting—presumably a nude—which has been modestly covered with a throwcloth. The whole exposition is charming: innocent, historically not very important, and quite delightful.

Two shows of the Belgian Surrealist Magritte are also on view, one at the Bodley Gallery of his drawings, the other at Iolas of his paintings. Magritte's work is the type example of "magic realism"; the painting is clear, simple, and almost offensively banal, the ideas depicted elaborately obscure, and the titles completely mystifying. Why, for example, should a painting of a glass of water atop an open umbrella be called *Les Vacances de Hegel,* or a chair out of whose seat grows a lion's tail be called *Une Simple Histoire d'Amour?* A stone interior with a stone man in a stone Prince Albert, with a stone lion at his feet and on the wall a stone picture signed "Magritte" is *Souvenir de Voyage,* while the Tower of Pisa leaning against a feather is *La Nuit de Pise.* The only title making any work-a-day sense is that of a picture of a tree in summer dusk, in front of whose black foliage appears the crescent moon. This is called *Le 16 Septembre,* apparently the date on which it was finished.

The images in the pictures are provocative and difficult to forget. The painting technique is less engaging. But this naïve paint surface and sign-painter's drawing style are unquestionably deliberate, intended to render more piquant the high sophistication of the riddles. Perhaps the joke is carried a little far. The drawings shown at the Bodley have the same subjects as the oils. Without the heavy-handed paint, they are more direct and pleasing. But of the oils, only *Le 16 Septembre,* with its convincing picture postcard version of approaching night, is seriously interesting as painting.

Magic Realism such as this, with its careful edges and overall neatness, may seem at first sight very near to the *trompe l'oeil* tradition of Raphaelle Peale's "deceptions." Actually, nothing could be more different. *Trompe l'oeil,* if it wishes to deceive the eye, must also deceive binocular vision. Consequently it is limited to painting shallow space. It can take as subjects only those without recession—such as letters in a rack or objects hanging on a door—and paint them as if lying close behind the canvas. *Trompe l'oeil* is a frivolous form of still life, and its tight drawing and concealed brushwork are simply further aids to the deception.

Magic Realism, on the other hand, is a serious form of fantasy painting, differing from other fantasy painting only in that it attempts to endow the dream world which is its subject with a convincing air of concrete reality. For this effect it sometimes imitates photography—which our time is prone to mistake for visual reality itself—and paints with the all-over sharpness seen by a stopped-down lens. Or it takes advantage of the common symbols for reality to be found in naïve painting. Actually, the visual reality the painter sees is much too complex for the camera's simple vision, or for the naïve painter's limited formulas. Which is probably why Magic Realist painting often seems either over-elaborate or devitalized, and this despite the fascination of its underlying poetic ideas.

# *Brooklyn Bridge, Whitney Friends and the Guggenheim International*

THE BROOKLYN Museum is holding an anniversary exhibition in honor of the seventy-fifth birthday of the Brooklyn Bridge. There are paintings, photographs, newspaper engravings, engineering drawings, and even a massive two-foot section of the suspension cable—quite enough to tempt one to cross the bridge to see.

The best-known of the paintings are those by Joseph Stella, of which the earliest, painted in 1918 on a bed sheet, is the finest. Of the two Albert Gleizeses, the one painted in 1917 is almost the handsomest bright-colored Synthetic Cubist explosion I have ever seen. There is a charming primitive by Israel Litwak in varnished colored crayon with things glued on, a false primitive by Guglielmi of a South Street wedding, an Afro, an O'Keeffe, a Hassam, a Marin, a Saul Steinberg and a Hedda Sterne. There is lacking only Eugène Berman's drawing of some years back—probably inappropriate for an anniversary celebration—of the bridge in ruins.

The bridge itself took sixteen years to build. It cost the life of its designer, John Augustus Roebling, and rendered his son an invalid. It was completed in 1883. Its massive design, so characteristic of the architecture of that decade, is evident even in the engineering plans displayed. These nostalgic proportions, as well as the bridge's reassuring durability, have made it an object of affection for us all. It is our Eiffel Tower.

The Whitney Museum has on show one hundred eighty pictures and pieces of sculpture loaned by members of the Friends of the Whitney Museum of American Art—a representative selection of the American work of the last fifty years, both Abstract and Representational, from Henri and Sloan to Rivers and Hofmann. Although the pictures come from private collections, their execution is in general more brilliant and their subjects more striking than one would think a domestic interior could comfortably accept. Such bright restlessness is one of the common characteristics of present-day American painting, but it is certainly not found in Jack Levine's wonderful *King,* crowned and reading a torah, in Mark Tobey's *Travellers III,* with its sprinkling of pale, square dots, in any of the Marins, in Glackens' *March Day in Washington Square,* with its lovely spring color, in the unexpectedly beautiful Eilshemius *Boat and Inlet,* in Isabel Bishop's man *Mending,* or in the *May V* of John Levee with its handsome, thick, dry, paint surface. Among the more public and aggressive works, Ivan Albright's *The Hole in the Wall Gang,* a still life of a suit of cowboy clothes, is particularly fine, as is Reginald Marsh's *Steeplechase Park,* crowded with laughing girls being tossed about in fun machines, the painter's wife standing amused and happy in their midst.

The Friends of the Whitney Museum is organized to further the welfare of contemporary American painting. It is going about it by the only effective method yet devised—by buying works of art. Its purpose is incomparably more respectable than that of the preceding Whitney exhibition—Twentieth Century American Painting in Reproduction. This was a showing of forty color reproductions assembled by the United States Information Agency, three hundred identical sets of which, mounted and labeled, are to be distributed among the U. S. embassies and agencies abroad.

However good its intentions, the U.S.I.A., in distributing reproductions of paintings, is not supporting art, it is encouraging lip service; it is not patronizing artists, but underwriting publishers. Popularizing color prints does not sell paintings. Even the small royalties accruing from the sale of the reproductions go to the collectors and museums that own the pictures, not to the men who made them. Other governments interested, as all governments are, in the advancement of national culture provide their embassies with real works of art. We do not furnish our foreign offices with imitation ice boxes and fake Cadillacs. Why should we provide them with fake pictures?

The Solomon R. Guggenheim Museum is showing the winners and runners-up of the first of its annual national and international prize competitions. While I do not believe that this exhibit furnishes a complete description of all kinds of contemporary painting, it can nevertheless be taken as a description of the kinds of painting which receive prizes in this decade. To win a prize in the seventies a picture had to relate an anecdote, usually one containing a female nude. In the 1910's, a Renaissance composition or a Pointillist technique was necessary—preferably both. Today, to win a prize, a picture should be large and free of references to the visual world. If, however, an image is presented, this image must serve only as a supporting framework for some painting trick which is in reality the picture's subject. The trick is usually one of paint texture or of paint application, like dripping or painting with a six-inch brush; perhaps a self-imposed trademark, like using only black and white; or it may be a trick of stylistic reference—to disassociative Cubism, or to mechanical drawing, or to children's painting. The importance of the image is thus minimized and the picture is rendered neutral and inoffensive. The trick provides exhibition brilliance and the large size gives museum importance.

I do not wish to imply that the pictures in the present exhibition are not striking and for the most part strikingly handsome. I only question their ability to hold our interest for any length of time. Indeed, of the international prize winner painted by Ben Nicholson, I can remember only that it was pale color, painted on what appeared to be a gesso preparation, and contained some neat black curves.

# *Marin and Shahn*

FORTY EARLY paintings by the late John Marin in water color, oil, and pastel, all done before 1920, the painter's fiftieth year, are on view at the Downtown Gallery. Marin is the most celebrated of the American water-colorists. Since 1909, when he was first shown here by Stieglitz, his reputation has steadily grown. The Museum of Modern Art gave him a retrospective exhibit in 1936, many years before his death, and in its recent historical survey of great American painters the Metropolitan assigned him a major place. His oils have not been universally admired, but he is accepted as the most original, vigorous, and inventive of water-colorists. The remarkable flatness of the present show comes as a great surprise.

The subject of these pictures is New York buildings, Paris and Tyrol landscape, and the coast of Maine. The more mature work employs a twisting perspective based on a multiple point of view, a perspective system derived, if not directly from Delaunay's teetering views of the Eiffel Tower, at any rate from parallel Futurist sources. This kinetic system, at first applied only to the objects and buildings depicted, is later extended to become the zigzag grillwork so often imposed on the picture itself and the polygonal inner frame which has become a Marin trademark. The painting technique itself derives from the faceted pencil outlines and fragmented color washes of the Cézanne water-color drawings, but executed in the rapid, slapdash brushwork and rough, dry paper of Homer, Sargent and the other water-color virtuosi.

This lightness of hand in Marin has always been particularly admired, as well as the atmospheric charm of his color. In the pictures here the color is thin and flat. The constant presence of white paper, left uncovered by the water-color washes, grays every tone to a flabby uniformity. The oils, done on the same water-color system with a putty-colored canvas showing through, are dry and without warmth. As for the hand, it is so invariably light as to appear skittish, and the pictures themselves frivolous, mannered and without conviction. Only a very few have forms with enough pictorial interest to be remembered.

All this is very curious. Perhaps Marin's better work of this period was not available or the pictures were not properly selected. It may be that the vigor for which Marin is so well known is paled by the athleticism of our contemporaries, or that his invention suffers in comparison with the skill and variety of the Homer water colors I have so recently seen. Perhaps, as is more likely, Marin was best after fifty. A show of the later pictures, from 1920 to 1953, is promised by the same gallery for a later date. It will be interesting to find out whether this work is as spectacular as one remembers, whether one is remembering the work itself or one of the most spectacular merchandising campaigns in recent history.

Eighteen works by Ben Shahn, in water-color, ink, and tempera, are on show at the same gallery. Shahn's highly personal painting is almost too well known to describe; according to the catalogue, examples are owned by fifty-two museums in America and one in Australia. His pictures are bright, flat, and semisatiric, in a style which evokes the painting of children. The line is dry and brittle, with something of the acrid wit of Klee, Grosz, and Steinberg. The composition, enormously elegant, is based on oddity of shape. The drawing is of the symbolic type in which five fingers with nails denote a hand. The color is beautiful.

The subjects of the present show are a great deal less biting than one expects: musicians play jazz; a man contemplates a molecular diagram; one called *Cosmos* shows two rich gentlemen, possibly capitalists, and a bunch of flowers; in *Conversation,* two men, having removed their masks, converse. It is all forceful enough but about generalities, full of references to science and the humanities. There are atoms and molecular structures, phoenixes in flame and mathematical expressions for the space-time continuum—all good decorative motifs. The pictures themselves are decorative, a little wry perhaps, and a little thin.

The room below contains a selection of Shahn's prints, among them, presumably an earlier one, of Sacco and Vanzetti in chains —intense, noble, thin, and terribly pathetic. Then I saw why I was disappointed. Ben Shahn is the most wonderful political caricaturist of our time. He has gone respectable.

# Some Americans and Others

THE WHITNEY is holding a fourfold exhibit—the painters Karl Knaths and Abraham Rattner and the sculptors Doris Caesar and Chaim Gross—under the title of Four American Expressionists. Each separate group of work is large and comprehensive, each contains more than thirty examples and represents the work of twenty to thirty years. The artists themselves are highly respected and enjoy considerable following. My only complaint is a personal one. I do not find their work particularly sympathetic.

Of the four artists, Doris Caesar is the least remarkable. Her sculpture is of two kinds—small story-telling groups, and larger single, elongated female figures, generally nudes. The groups are not very different from Bavarian peasant wood-carving—though they are superior in workmanship—and the single figures seem expressive of little but exaggerated self-pity. The other sculptor, Chaim Gross, is more engaging. His *Easter Sunday*—a young woman proud of her new hat—has the naïve charm of an early American ship's figurehead, and the *Young Mother,* clothed, thin, and pregnant, is very touching. The greater part of his work, however, consists of stylized female acrobats, usually twined into garlands. These pieces with their multiple doll-like faces and bumpy bottoms, so reminiscent of the Rose O'Neill Kewpies of my childhood, look exactly like well-filled Christmas stockings.

As for the painters, Karl Knaths can paint very handsome canvases in rich, effective color. Witness his *Frightened Deer in Moonlight* and his *Clam Diggers, Provincetown* of 1949. But in most of his pictures the vigor of his original idea is lost, and its expressivity muffled, in the systematic abstraction he imposes. This stylization is found in all the work. He uses no colors but a small predetermined group of tones prepared in advance and employed without intermixture. There are no lines except straight ones and the simplest of curves. And these he superposes in Cubist-style patterns on his color areas. This uniform and limiting procedure renders most of his canvases thin and posterlike. In a group they are monotonous.

Abraham Rattner is a more varied painter. Certainly nothing of Knaths' here shown is as original as Rattner's *Window Cleaner No. 1* with its spider man almost as transparent as the window he is cleaning. But Rattner's color is in the taste of my aunt from the country who used to say, "I don't like things to be gaudy. All I want is plenty of red, blue, green, purple, and yaller." At any rate all of these colors at highest intensity appear in each of his pictures. And with his stock of Clowns, Masks, Christs, and Don Quixotes, he of all our contemporaries seems the most given to self-pity—a wailing wall indeed. Recalling the word "Expressionist" in the title of the present exhibition, one is tempted to suspect that to express self-pity is what Expressionism means. Though it is difficult to see how Gross, a naïve charmer, and Knaths, a Cubist-formed Abstractionist, could qualify as Expressionists no matter how the definition were framed. Be that as it may, the show is extaordinarily well done, and for their many admirers, the works have probably never been so well presented.

More complex and considerably more pleasing is the work by Bernard Dufour at Albert Loeb. These large, easy, bright pictures, loosely painted on a white ground in lively, harmonious colors, contain no recognizable images. But unlike most current non-objective paintings, Dufour's are not easy to dismiss as decoration. The execution has a conviction, the strokes and tones a subtlety and variety usually to be found only in the most skillful and economical depiction of real and visible objects. The painting is neither capricious nor affected. It firmly states. The effect is of someone talking quite slowly and clearly in a language one does not understand. I have not the slightest idea what is being said, but I am convinced of the logic. Perhaps these pictures—like certain Cubist pictures or some of Cézanne's water colors which become clear only when the subject is divined—depict the familiar world but do it with unfamiliar simplifications or from an unfamiliar point of view. One finds hints in the work of landscape seen from above, and of highly enlarged plants or amoebas. Perhaps, on the contrary, the pictures are a rigorous exposition of an essentially hermetic field, like the work of Marcel Duchamp. Or perhaps, in spite of the beauty of hand displayed, the conviction itself is only another stylistic device and the pictures another example of contemporary decoration. The only way to find out would be to see the pictures more often. I feel quite sure one will.

The American Academy of Arts and Letters is showing eighty-five canvases, ranging from Whistler to Marin, chosen to illustrate the Impressionist Mood in American Painting. Childe Hassam, the most fecund of these painters, is represented by only three canvases, the large collection owned by the Institute itself not having been gone into. But the show includes a number of paintings by Theodore Robinson, a charming and quite unknown contemporary of Hassam who died before the end of the century—gray-green pictures in sober taste, of which a moonlight scene of 1892 is one of the handsomest canvases shown. In addition there are: a black and white sketch by Sargent of an orchestra rehearsing, done in 1876 when the painter was twenty; a number of Twachtmans and some Bellowes; a John Sloan of New York seen from the Palisades; two brilliant beach scenes by Gifford Beal; a Glackens and a Marsh, both of crowds, hung side by side, which turn out to be extraordinarily alike save that the Glackens is red and blue while the Marsh is tan and brown. The group also contains two limpid, open views of Long Island seaside by William M. Chase; and a particularly good Cubist still life by Alfred Maurer.

The tenor of the show is gentle and pastoral. The pictures are well chosen, the painting straightforward and expressive. One feels little of the breath-taking grandeur to be found in French Impressionism; on the other hand, there is none of the corn and sentiment of German and Italian Impressionism and none of the restless virtuosity that Impressionism acquired when transplanted to Spain. The pictures seem to have been done with pleasure. One can see in them the enormous liberation offered to painters by these new methods of systematic improvisation. If on the whole the effect is somewhat dry, that is principally, I think, because the painters seem so little interested in people. In these pictures nature is the principal actor. Man, when he appears, is either a characterizing local coloration, as in the beach scenes by Beal; a decorative motif, as in Davies or Prendergast, or a subject for caricature, as in Hart, March, or Glackens. This, of course, is not unexceptionally true, but compared to the rich humanity of French Impressionism, the American wing seems more than a little remote.

Absence of humanity cannot be charged against the twenty-seven paintings of the nude by Jules Pascin, on view at Perls. This is Pascin at his best and on his favorite subject—*la petite femme* of Paris artist and café life, presented as she is: tough, young, impersonal, professional, and available. Girls like these, but prettified, are the standard theme of the frivolous French painters from Boucher to the illustrators for *La Vie Parisienne*. Pascin had the extraordinary quality to take them seriously, seeing their strong little bodies without sentiment or glamour, with only understanding and perhaps desire. His pictures of them are touching and human, erotic and at the same time curiously noble. These are single or double figures, or rather portraits, the faces firmly characterized but without expression, the flesh soft and roundly modeled without any stylization whatever. The painting is very thin—washes of color that scarcely cover the rapid shorthand outlines by which the pictures were begun. The hand is astonishingly sure, the drawing solid, expert and easy. In spite of the limited subject, this is some of the finest work the School of Paris has produced. And it is a pleasure in a time of lofty, esthetic theories and High-style Abstraction to be faced with a painter who had a taste for the routine and more commonly appreciated things of life.

The highest of the High-style Abstractionism I have yet encountered is the group of paintings by Adolph Gottlieb on view at the Andre Emmerich Gallery. This show consists of seven large, vertical, and unframed canvases, each, as nearly as I could judge, some four feet broad by eight feet high and each a slight variation on the identical theme. The canvas is white. In the top section a roughly oval spot is painted in some rich dark color, while the lower section contains a more irregular splotch in another dark color or in black. The effect is extremely stylish. When I was there the place was empty except for one other visitor, an elegantly dressed, handsome and rather worried-looking woman as impatient as a model waiting for the photographer. Perhaps she was. The pictures would be perfect as backgrounds for fashion photography. It is difficult to conceive of other use for them. Almost no house has so large a vertical area of wall whose lower part is not already occupied by fireplace, chair or table. This sort of problem seems to bother even the Betty Parsons Gallery whose present exhibition of similar, though not vertical, pictures is entitled Paintings for Unlimited Space.

The most entertaining exhibit in town is the Kinetic Sculpture of George Rickey shown at Kraushaar. These are elaborately and beautifully made machines for doing nothing. Constructed of aluminum, brass, and piano wire, balanced and counter-balanced with watchmakers' precision, they spin and turn and dip at the slightest breath or touch. Some are even activated by air currents set up by the spectator's approach. I have never seen among the art-mobiles such pretty toys. Another amusing exhibit is the group of twelve collages and constructions by various artists at the Alan Gallery. They are witty, elaborate and surprisingly varied. *Hotel de l'Etoile,* for example, by Joseph Cornell in his usual impeccable workmanship is a little white peep-show with a background of a sky and stars; Jasper John presents *Three Flags,* all American and superimposed in diminishing sizes; *The Walk* by Bruce Gilchrist is a plaque of tar in which is embedded precious-seeming objects such as opened-up beer cans with the golden insides showing and discarded radio tubes; and Bruce Conner's *Collage* has two surfaces, the front covered with assorted textures and materials, the back with pin-up girls and cut-out photographs of nudes. This thoroughly delightful show bears a somewhat pretentious title. It is called "Beyond Painting."

Whether the work is beyond painting in the sense that it has surpassed it, I would not venture to decide. But certainly this exhibit has nothing in common with painting except the occasional presence of paint. Painting and this are different games, played with quite different rules. The basis of painting is visual ideas; deprived of images it does not exist. This other practice has no need for images whatever. It uses the motor and visceral emotions aroused by texture, handwork, and the visible evidence of muscular effort to generate the sentiments of luxury, elegance, and surprise. I have no objection to calling it an art. It is the work of talented and dedicated people. But I do not see how by any stretch of the imagination it can be classed with painting.

# *Art Auction*

FIFTY WORKS of modern art, donated by artists, dealers, and collectors, were auctioned late last month for the benefit of the Museum of Modern Art's thirtieth-anniversary fund. This sale, at the Parke-Bernet Galleries in New York, was easily the most brilliant event of the season. The audience was made up of all the prominent figures in selling, collecting, and curating modern art. The Mayor, Mr. Wagner himself, was there, and the ceremony was introduced by Mrs. John D. Rockefeller III. The multiple Leicas of some fifteen press photographers flashed incessantly to record it, while the crews of two television cameras transmitted the scene by closed circuit to bidders in Dallas, Chicago, and Los Angeles. The bidding, in behalf of a respected cause, was brisk and cheerful. The ladies' hats, like large, tight bouquets of fresh spring flowers, were wonderful, and the auctioneer, Mr. Louis Marion, in front of a pink curtain and lit by rosy spots, was the best of television entertainment.

The works being auctioned had been selected by Alfred Barr, Jr., director of the museum's collections, from those offered to the museum for the occasion. Apart from two Cézannes and three Renoirs, they were all by the names in modern art, from Braque and Picasso to Soulage and Mathieu, which are the museum's special province. The over-all quality of the collection was disappointing. In fact, there were only two pieces of first quality among the entire fifty. The finest, given by Governor Nelson Rockefeller, was a quite wonderful Braque *Violon* in the high Cubist manner of 1913; the other a Picasso pastel, one of the best, depicting, in his 1920 "Neo-Classical" style with daring and skillful distortions, a pair of meditative and affectionate female nudes. Of the two Cézannes, the more important—a characteristic still life with wall-paper, apples, and crumpled napkin—was one of his more heavy-handed pieces, while the other—three small dead birds on a brick-red cloth—was a minor work and unappealing. As for the three Renoirs, only one had any pictorial quality, and that—a late painting of a large fat servant—was singularly unattractive. The Juan Gris was characteristic but not his best, and I have seen better Pascins. Morandi and Dubuffet were represented by good examples of their work—of the first a sparse *Vase of Flowers* and of the other a *Jazz Band*. There was a charming and somewhat posterish Tamayo of a night sky with moon and hills and constellation of stars; an important Miró; a Gorki, thin but with pretty color. Apart from these, almost everything was either unimportant snips or, in my opinion, decidedly second rate.

Nevertheless, the auction netted the museum almost $900,000. The highest prices were paid for the Cézanne still life—$200,000—and for the Braque *Violon* which brought $145,000. ("That's not a price," said Mr. Marion, the auctioneer. "You can't stop there. Think how much nicer to be able to say 'That picture cost me $150,000!' ") The large Renoir went for $31,000, which I understand is something less than the usual market for a Renoir of that size, and the Picasso pastel brought in $32,000. The bidding for one of the works—a large energetic crisscrossing of black paint on a brown ground by Hartung—was stopped by a precisionist in the audience who protested that it was being displayed upside down. The bidding was resumed and the picture, still upside down, went for $11,000; a pair of negligible Matisse paper cutouts went as one of the cheapest lots for $2,600.

The prices, I am given to understand by dealer friends, were not exaggerated: slightly higher than the market, perhaps, on some of the smaller pieces, and lower than expected on some of the more important ones, but roughly comparable to what the works would have cost from a dealer. They seem, nonetheless, for the most part astonishingly out of scale with the pieces' real value as works of art, and are more than a little shocking to one like myself, not a dealer or collector, but a painter, accustomed to evaluate work on its own qualities rather than on the publicity rating of the painter's name. It almost seemed—as it has seemed before—that the buyers were collecting signatures rather than pictures.

Just the same, such prices are standard for work, even indifferent work, by famous-name painters of today. There are several reasons for it. To begin with, and contrary to received opinion, successful contemporary painters have always brought higher prices than old masters—except those few outstanding masterpieces from the past which only rarely turn up in the market. In any given period, contemporary work is more in demand. Naturally enough; we would find it on the whole more cheerful to live with a Matisse, say, than with a Rembrandt. And if we are astonished at the prices commanded by Braque or Picasso, remember the prices brought by Bougereau or Meissonier in the nineties and by Sargent and Lazlo in the years before the wars. And high prices even for painters whose names have worn better than these were also normal. In the sale of Degas' collection, which took place in 1918 in Paris under bombardment by the German guns—certainly not the most favorable background for a public auction—a small Cézanne of two green apples brought $2,000, a tiny *Bathers* $5,000 and a Manet $10,000.

However, another factor operates today to inflate the picture market. Under our income tax regulations, a deduction (up to thirty per cent of taxable income) is allowed for donations to schools, hospitals, or charities. In this context a museum counts as a charitable institution, and if it accepts a work of art, the work's money value can be listed by the donor as a tax deduction. The money value of a picture is at the best a guess, depending on highly subjective estimates of what it would bring if sold on the public market. It is to the donor's advantage—and not to the disadvantage of the museum—to assess the value of his gift as high as possible. All of this tends to jack up the prices of pictures, particularly of pictures by famous names, which are, of course, what a museum will most willingly accept.

Up to a few years ago it was possible for a donor to announce his intention to give a picture to a museum, take its value off his income tax, and still remain in possession of the picture during his lifetime. This is no longer possible, though even now a museum may, after taking title to the picture, allow it to remain on loan at the donor's house. As a result, the market has for a number of years been ransacked for pictures acceptable to a museum, and sufficiently high in price to make the troublesome operation worth while. It is principally this which has been responsible for the astronomical prices museum-type pictures have now attained.

None of this applies directly to the recent auction. There the deductible value of the works contributed was not based on fanciful estimate, but on the exact amount each picture brought when sold. The high market was, of course, already established; the buyers, whatever their good will toward the museum, had no inducement to raise it higher. Furthermore, the pictures were offered to the Museum to sell at auction, not to hang in its own collection. Consequently, it could accept works of lower artistic merit than commonly appear in its galleries. This goes far to explain the group's low quality. That was not the museum's fault. The auction was announced; works were given; all the museum could do was to select the best. One remembers in this connection the Parisian doctor who was also a collector and whose collection was sharply divided into two categories. On the one hand were the excellent pictures he had bought himself. On the other were mediocre ones given him, in return for professional services, by his painter patients.

# MUSEUMS

# *Collectors, Taste in the Metropolitan, the New York Museums of Decoration and Primitive Art*

THE METROPOLITAN Museum has opened its new south wing galleries with an exhibit of paintings, furniture, and objects from its permanent collection, grouped under their original donors' names. The pieces themselves are well known; they are among the finest the museum possesses. Their present rearrangement, introduced by some contemporary photographs of the donors' mansions, offer a lively picture of tastes and personalities.

The taste of Henry G. Marquand, in 1881 second president of the museum, must have been sober, rich, accurate, and firmly conservative. His pictures, principally Dutch or Flemish, are of the very first quality. There is a Vermeer, a Hals, a Rembrandt, a Van Dyck of an English lord. Mr. Marquand's solid, advanced-conservative position can be divined from a set of extraordinary Greek-Victorian furniture, of ebony inlaid with ivory and moonstones, designed by Alma Tadema and Sir Frederick Leighton. A room in his house where this furniture was used contained among other things three classical busts, an inscription from Aeschylus, a tiger-skin rug, a Grecian grand piano mounted on sphinxes and Alma Tadema's *Reading from Homer*. If one can judge from the photograph, it was all very sumptuous as well as appropriate in the home of a rich and cultivated gentleman brought up on the classics.

The selection from the Morgan collection has quite a different character. J. Pierpont Morgan, I have been given to understand, did not collect pieces; he collected collections. His acquisitions were so numerous that he could never see them together; they were scattered in his various houses, in storage, and on loan to museums. To judge from the works on display, his attitude toward art was that of an owner. The character common to all these pieces is their fabulous value. They are more imposing for their craftsmanship, materials, or rarity than for their human communication. Everything is rich. There are gold-plate and ivory statuettes, tapestries and carvings, and great public monuments like the Colonna altar piece by Raphael or the parade helmet of Francis the First of France —all easier to esteem as artistic rarities than to love as works of art. In the field of collecting, Mr. Morgan was more a conquistador than an aficionado.

The Vanderbilt and Blumenthal rooms have characters equally revealing. The Vanderbilt collection, with its Rembrandt, Gainsborough, and Reynolds, and its black lacquer *chinoiserie* cabinets made for Marie Antoinette, seems less like an art collection than like the dismantled furnishings of a great English house—precisely the great house, as I have been told, the Vanderbilts considered themselves to be. And the Blumenthal collection brings to mind the stage. George Blumenthal was a banker and financier. His house at Park and 70th Street was built in the style of a Florentine palazzo. Almost everything it contained in the way of decoration was what a Renaissance prince might have inherited or acquired. His collection, with its Gothic furniture and mille-fleurs tapestries, seems more like the materials for a lavish stage set than like a collection of art. Even the Joos van Gent *Adoration of the Magi,* the most pretentious picture here, has a curious air of being a conscientious copy of some tempera original run up in oil on canvas for a stage occasion. And one receives the not unsympathetic impression of Mr. Blumenthal playing against this grandiose background the role of Medici banker-prince.

The Havemayer rooms give a different impression altogether. Mr. and Mrs. H. O. Havemayer left Philadelphia for Paris in the seventies. They had an eye. Also, the painter, Mary Cassatt, was their intimate friend. It was perhaps through her that they became so promptly aware of the great Impressionists and of the art of Japan that had then begun to delight advanced French taste. They bought extensively and well, each purchase a gem—the best of Greco, Degas, Goya, Corot—some of the finest pictures in the world. The best, and the most, of the Japanese screens in the museum's extensive collection (two are shown here) as well as some fourteen hundred other oriental objects come from this source.

But here is a curious thing. The Havemayer collection tells us nothing at all about the Havemayers' social ambitions or how they regarded themselves. The objects they acquired are all too good for this. One learns only that they had advanced taste, independence of mind, a passion for painting, and a talent for discovery. Their pictures have human size. They were made to communicate, not to overwhelm. They were bought to be lived with. They tell their own story, not their collectors'.

Something of collectors' taste can also be seen at the small new Museum of Contemporary Crafts on 53rd Street in a display—called The Patron Church—of modern ecclesiastical architecture and decorative arts. The architecture exhibit—models and photographs of both buildings and projects—forms the most interesting part of the show. Modern architecture has seldom made quite satisfactory churches. They are too frequently conceived in a manner more appropriate to exhibition booths in a world's fair—as was the famous Church of Pampulha by the Brazilian architect Niemeyer, which the Bishop of Bello Horizonte refused to consecrate. But here for the most part the buildings seem endowed with space, quiet, and dignity; to mention only the Kneses Tifereth Israel Synagogue at Port Chester, New York, by Philip Johnson with its ingeniously-hung vaulted ceiling and rows of vertical slits which constitute its colored windows; the Kresge Chapel at the Massachusetts Institute of Technology, with its pendant acoustical dampers; the Congregation Beth El Synagogue at South Orange, New Jersey, with its elaborately decorative detail; and the Chapel of the Holy Cross at Sedona, Arizona, poised on a barren cliff-side, opening to the desert sky.

The art objects displayed—hangings, vestments, windows, decorative plaques, devotional sculpture, and liturgical implements—are handsome and severely modern. The greater part are done in the contemporary non-objective manner—safe and careful arrangements of colors, shapes, and textures. These are the best—rich, decorative, and impersonal. Those in which some representation of the human face or figure appears seem either malicious and caricature, or sentimental and mawkish. Whether this is the fault of artist or patron is hard to say. Perhaps our present day art training deals more easily with the complexities of texture than with the mysteries of spirit. Perhaps the contemporary church can no longer accept from artists that curious mixture of tenderness and irony which gave the works it formerly patronized their touching reality and human scale. At any rate, to judge from this exhibition, the injunction "thou shalt make no graven image" seems for the churches today a very salutary measure.

Nearby on 54th Street, another small and new institution—The Museum of Primitive Art—is showing some sixty objects chosen from its permanent collection, which consists principally of a splendid group of primitive art objects assembled and donated by Nelson A. Rockefeller. The pieces now displayed come from cultures all over the world. About half are nineteenth- and twentieth-century Australian, African, and Melanesian; half are pre-Columbian from the two Americas; one is from Japan. The objects are extremely handsome—to mention only a ghost mask from French Equatorial Africa in carved wood painted white; two ominous Grade Society figures from the New Hebrides; and a vessel in the form of a badger from a mound in Arkansas. The lighting and presentation could not be better. Some slight ethnological background is furnished along with the catalogue, but ethnology is not the theme of this show. The presentation of so many diverse objects in one collection, as though they were part of a common tradition, removes their original meaning. Religious and magic implications are ignored, and we are invited to admire them solely as works of art, as if they were by contemporary artists working in the Primitive style.

The slightly disturbing thing in such a presentation is the tacit assumption that there is a Primitive style. Actually, a Neo-Primitive style does exist, as distinct a style as Byzantine or modern. It consists of the contemporary work done with stylistic references to some Primitive art. But there is no such thing as a style common to all Primitive arts. They are much too diverse for this, containing as they do the whole pre-history of mankind. What Mr. Rockefeller, long associated with modern art, has assembled is a most valuable collection of indigenous objects which have resemblances to Modern art or might possibly inspire it.

# *Baltimore, Raleigh, and Sarasota*

IT HAS recently been my pleasure, traveling south, to visit the Cone collection in the Baltimore Museum, the new Museum of Art at Raleigh, North Carolina, and the Ringling Museum in Sarasota, Florida. The pictures are well worth seeing; even more interesting is the character of the collections themselves. For, just as the quality of the pictures in a collection demonstrates the collector's taste, so also the sort of pictures collected indicates the purpose they were intended to serve.

The Cone collection consists of works by Impressionist and Modern painters. Dr. Claribel and Miss Etta Cone were women of independent mind and assured and sensitive taste. They had met Picasso and Matisse as early as 1905, long before the famous Armory show brought Modern art to American attention. Their pictures were acquired usually in Paris, often with the painter's advice, sometimes from the painter himself. They bought for their own pleasure, for their own use, for their own home, solely because they liked pictures. Consequently, their collection is all of a piece. There are many charming and intimate works, few dominating exhibition pieces, and almost no inferior examples. It is, so to speak, a "domestic" collection, made to be lived with. The museum rooms seem to retain some of the charm the Cone house once certainly possessed.

The work of Matisse, their life-long friend, forms the principal part of the collection—some forty canvases, a number of small bronzes and many drawings and prints. The works date from 1895 through 1947 and include examples of all the painter's styles; the early still lifes not unlike Bonnard, *The Blue Nude* of his Fauve period—a large, crude picture, probably intended as an exhibition shocker and here somewhat out of place—a considerable number of the small landscapes and interiors with figures of the early twenties—by far the most pleasing group—as well as some of the larger, brighter, thinner pictures of his later manner. It is the most sympathetic presentation of Matisse I have yet seen, showing him as a calm and workmanlike painter in the late Impressionist tradition, not too unlike Bonnard or Vuillard, using for subject matter, as do so many of the good French from Chardin down, the painter's domestic life. Here, reduced to domestic size, he appears more human and more congenial than in the large, professional, and impersonally decorative work by which we know him best.

"Matisse and his Period" the collection might be called, for almost everybody is here, from Corot to Max Weber, and in good examples. Of Cézanne there are two of the best—a wonderful

*Mte. Ste. Victoire* and a most engaging small *Bathers.* There is a beautiful Gauguin, a Tahitian woman in a violet robe, an unusually handsome landscape by Derain with sunbaked southern fields and olive trees, and a fine picture by Theodore Robinson, an American Impressionist, of a little girl on a wood path practicing her violin.

Picasso is represented by a few oils and many drawings and studies, almost all done in the early 1900's. There is in particular a study in gouache and pastel of some of his circus characters—of the fat man in red tights and a ruff, with the thin little boy leaning against his knee. The most important oil shown—the well-known *Mother and Child* of 1922 in his Neo-Classic manner—is in reality a drawing, not a painting at all. Examining the canvas, one can see that the painter began in color with pink flesh, white dress, a blue coat on the child, and a background of green landscape or leaves. Then, dissatisfied with what he had done, he effaced it all, leaving only areas of color. On these, with a brush dipped in brown, he redrew his sketch. The picture, never carried out in paint, remains a drawing in line on a tinted background, an example of how this artist is able so frequently to escape the problems of oil paintings by a brilliant and charming trick.

The collection at Raleigh has another character altogether. The museum there is quite new, created recently by an act of the North Carolina legislature, and housed in a handsome new building next to the capitol. The greater part of the collection was bought with state funds by a local committee headed by Dr. W. R. Valentiner, the Museum's director. The purpose of the collection is public and didactic—to attract tourists and to disseminate knowledge of art. Consequently, the collection contains many large pictures and many great names. The paintings are highly varnished, in good repair and obviously of immense value. Few of them are possible to imagine in a private home. One is struck by the importance given to English portraiture, to Rubens and his school, and by the many large and unwieldy pictures with biblical subjects, the most extraordinary example of this official painting being a picture of Joan of Arc at prayers, by Rubens, whose greatest interest lies in the improbable concurrence of the two names.

Fortunately the collection is large and contains more and much handsomer pictures than these. I can mention only a small Jan Breughel, a harbor scene with fish, boats, and hundreds of people, whose pretext is some embarkation of St. Paul's; a magnificent collection of Dutch and Spanish still lifes; a group of seventeenth-century Italian landscapes of city architecture; and a particularly fine early Tiepolo of Cleopatra drinking her pearl. One is grateful, too, for the many nineteenth-century Americans. It is time someone began to bring them out.

The Ringling collection has something of a mixed character, being a private collection, taken over by a state authority and reorganized by a curator of highly individual tastes. It consists principally of the pictures acquired by John Ringling, who had a passion—one would like to think of it as a circus owner's delight in showmanship—for large and opulent works of art. For these he built a statue-studded Italianate palazzo, as large and opulent as the pictures themselves, and willed it all to Florida. For ten years after his death the museum remained closed, but in 1946 the state appointed the late A. Everett Austin, Jr., of the Hartford Athenaeum as director.

Austin was a man of charm, energy, and originality, with a sure taste in pictures and a profound knowledge of the theater. It was he who was responsible for the original production in Hartford of *Four Saints in Three Acts,* the Stein-Thomson opera. His specialty, Baroque painting, as well as his talent as a showman made him particularly suited for Sarasota. The Ringling paintings, after a decade of neglect in the Florida climate, needed care and restoration. With the funds available, he made the necessary reparations and increased the collection with, among other things, a unique eighteenth-century theater brought complete from Asolo above Venice. Austin was a man of taste in the eighteenth-century sense of the word. He knew not only what to admire but how to buy, and whether he bought for himself or for his museum, it was to get something he himself valued and desired. Museums and collectors are often tempted to purchase relatively uninteresting pieces because of their educational value as characteristic works, or their investment value as rarities. Austin never was. His pleasure lay in buying pictures, not in adding names. And during his incumbency, the Sarasota Museum became, with its exhibitions, lectures, and concerts, the educational and cultural center of the state. His unexpected death earlier this year is everywhere deplored.

Thus the character of the present collection is due to Ringling, to Austin, and to the State of Florida. Many of the pictures bought by the circus owner are unexceptional masterpieces; for example, the four Rubens tapestry cartoons, the huge still life by Snyders, and the Veronese *Rest on the Flight into Egypt.* Some are merely opulent. The additions made by Austin, such as the imaginative landscapes by Monsù Desiderio or the delightful pictures of the Italian comedy, less important as names or values, are nonetheless of the highest quality. And for the part played in the collection by the State of Florida, one can suppose that the demands of art education and of the tourist trade are responsible for the retention of many inferior pictures, often more impressive as names than convincing as execution, and responsible as well for the overzealous removal, since Austin's death, of every trace of patina from the palazzo and its statuary. The museum is nevertheless still worth visiting.

And worth supporting too. One cannot overestimate the importance of these local museums in our cultural life. Knowledge about painting cannot be had from lectures or books or slides or reproductions. It must be acquired from actual pictures. Unlike recordings of music, the reproductions of pictures do not approximate the thing itself. They give little idea of the original's paint quality or color, nothing of its scale, and only a hint of its effect and communication. Only in museums such as these can young painters learn the possibilities of their trade, or can the people who do not live in great cities learn what painting is all about.

# *Brooklyn and Philadelphia*

It is a constant surprise to discover how different each museum is. The Metropolitan, for example, has a high, municipal opulence. The Frick is like a well-kept mansion on view in the owner's absence. The Philadelphia Museum, which I have recently visited, with its wealth of inherited private collections preserved intact, has something of the comfortable mustiness of the home of an elderly relative; while the Brooklyn Museum, more firmly departmentalized, calls to mind the beneficent efficiency and busy bareness of an educational institution or a public office.

Compared with Philadelphia, the Brooklyn Museum is not large. But its collections are easy to examine and extremely well selected. The Egyptian section is one of the finest in the country; even the Metropolitan has not its scope. The small French collection is representative and good, surprisingly good when one learns how long before their general appreciation these pictures were acquired. But the museum's great specialty is American painting. Its collection is big and constantly being enlarged, and ranges from the scrupulous, sign-painterly portraits of Colonial times to the eclecticisms of today. There is Gilbert Stuart's *George Washington* with its grandeur of pose, and its pretentiousness of background (columns, tassels, law books, and federal gold furniture) all done in the most vulgar of painting styles; Samuel Morse's *General Lafayette,* theatrically poised in front of storm and sunset under the approving eyes of the marble busts of Washington and Franklin; landscapes by Guy and Bierstadt, Cole and Cropsey; *The Last Days of Pompeii* of James Hamilton, smoldering in fire and ashes laid on with palette-knife; genre pieces by Mount and Bingham, Homer and Johnson; early Impressionism by Innes, Twachman and Robinson; many Ryders for those who like them; the finest Eakins; still lifes by Peale, Harnett, and Peto; Mary Cassatt, Sargent and Duvernick; the Ash Can School complete. Among the well-chosen examples of contemporaries—to mention only a few—Brooklyn owns a Marsh, a Raphael Soyer, a Marsden Hartley, a biting Jack Levine (an official dinner party called *Welcome Home*), a bridge by Hopper in quiet, distinguished color, and Larry Rivers' large, handsome, and expressive portrait of an old woman and two boys in *The Back Yard.* There are also the celebrated groups of water colors by Sargent and Winslow Homer.

It is somewhat disconcerting after this wealth of pictures to enter an enormous loft of period furniture arranged in severe rows like manufacturers' samples in a discount house; and to find plate glass, like the window fronts of a department store, protecting the representative series of Victorian rooms. But the displays themselves could not be more entertaining. A Louis XV salon from Saratoga with crystal gaslight chandeliers; a hall with scenic stained-glass windows from the old Marquand house at 68th and Madison; the sitting room from the John D. Rockefeller residence at 4 West 54th Street (by Eastlake in 1884) with spindle cornices and chair backs draped in tapestry, inspired by the Alhambra and more elegant than any Pullman car.

The framework of the museum on the whole is severe. One suspects that it is not rich in endowments. But sumptuous or not, the exhibits are well chosen, well displayed, and inventive. And when one considers the museum's art school, its collection of historical costumes, its Sunday concerts, and the character of its many special exhibitions—the famous Peto show for example, or the recent exhibit of American portraiture—it becomes apparent that the Brooklyn Museum acts less as a repository for precious objects than as a vigorous institution of public education operating intelligently with the funds at its disposal.

The Philadelphia Museum is much richer; it is indeed a storehouse of treasures. If the Brooklyn Museum has somewhat the dry organization of a department store, the Philadelphia, with its inherited collections, resembles an ancestral mansion enlarged by the heirs. It has a friendly, family air. The guards are amiable and the art students and young people one encounters seem both well mannered and completely at home. The museum's easy good will even affects the Picasso exhibition now being held. With a few changes—some extra Cubist pieces, more prints and drawings, and a show of ceramics—this is the same exhibit shown last summer in New York. But in Philadelphia, in the large, clear, well-lighted galleries, the pictures have a gaiety, a charm, a mocking and child-like wit that was little evident in the closed-in chambers and stern, doctrinaire atmosphere of the New York Museum of Modern Art.

The central armature of the Philadelphia Museum is a series of period rooms, complete with paintings, tapestry, woodwork, and furniture, arranged as if to be lived in, some even with the comfortable, well-worn look of present occupation. In addition, the museum has set up a series of architectural reconstructions—Romanesque and Gothic portals, a Spanish cloister, an Indian temple, the interior of a Chinese palace. In these rooms and courts are many of the museum's art objects and pictures. Three important collections, however, the John G. Johnson, the Gallatin, and the Arensberg, inherited and maintained as units, are exhibited in their own private quarters.

The Johnson collection was assembled in the great days of American collecting before the First World War. It is enormous. The catalogue claims some thirteen hundred pictures, from the early Italians to the Impressionists, but principally in the old-master categories. On the whole, I find them unrewarding. There are many excellent pieces, but the collection is uneven in quality and the pictures are not always in the best condition. Perhaps we no longer share the esthetic preoccupations which inspired their collection, for many seem more interesting as examples than convincing as masterpieces. I suspect, however, that the fault lies less with the pictures themselves than with their number. The collection is simply too large for effective display; it would be more impressive if more firmly edited.

The modern pictures are much more lively and arresting. The Gallatin and Arensberg collections, together with the other Modern works the museum displays, probably constitute the most important and representative assemblage of Modern art available in America.

A. E. Gallatin was an Abstract painter working in the flat, bright, angular style of the Cubist revival of the 1920's. He knew the Modern painters from having lived among them, and he bought pictures with a friend's opportunities and a painter's taste. His large collection—almost two hundred objects—is limited to the stricter and more schematic kinds of Abstract art, beginning with its first foreshadowing in the Cézanne water colors, through classical Cubism, and on to its fanciful or decorative developments by men such as Mondrian, Calder, and Miró. Most impressive is the number of early Cubist works by Picasso, Braque, and Juan Gris. There are few great museum pieces. The pictures are small and characteristic rather than large and important.

The Arensberg collection has a wider range; it does not ignore the representational aspect of Modern art. It is also incomparably richer in individually important works. Walter Arensberg was a brilliant and charming man, a very fine poet, I am told, as well, whose great passion—aside from the Baconian cipher—was Modern painting. Many of his pictures he bought as early as 1913, direct from the Armory Exhibit. Marcel Duchamp, the most hermetic of Modern painters and one of the greatest, advised his purchases. His collection is extraordinary. Besides a large pre-Columbian group there are some two hundred pieces of twentieth-century art, including all the principal sculptures of Brancusi and Duchamp's entire artistic output. One finds all three versions of the famous *Nude Descending a Staircase* and the equally famous plate glass window with lead and painted inserts entitled *The Bride Stripped Bare by Her Bachelors Even Marcel Duchamp,* as well as practically all the painter's early representational work and his mysterious jokes and "ready made" constructions, including a bird cage full of lump sugar and a glass bulb containing "one hundred cubic centimeters of the air of Paris, taken pure, before the arrival of the Germans."

There is an admirable group of early Braques, Picassos, and Grises; some of the finest Klees; a beautiful Rousseau of monkeys and jungle, and one of Dali's most effective and sinister monsters entitled *Soft Construction with Boiled Beans;* Chiricos, Mirós, Derains, Légers, Ernsts, as well as examples of painters one does not ordinarily see, like Picabia and Gleizes. Nothing, in fact, but what is exceptionally rare, exceptionally fine, or exceptionally interesting. No other single collection of Modern art I know has such variety and quality.

Collections even as fine as these are always something of a problem to a museum. They are the principal source of its pictures and must be unconditionally accepted. The real purpose of the gift, however, is to commemorate the donor, who insists that it be preserved intact. For as long as possible his wishes are observed. But the works themselves are more important than their grouping. Eventually, before anyone has realized it, the pictures have been rearranged, the uninteresting works have disappeared, schools are reunited, collections are coalesced, and the museum has achieved its real end—to present and describe not its benefactor's name and triumphs, but the history of art and the traditions of painting.

# *New England—Hartford, Northampton, Worcester, Springfield*

WISHING to see again some of the museums of New England, I profited by a week end in Massachusetts to visit the Wadsworth Athenaeum of Hartford, the Smith College Museum in Northampton, the Worcester Museum, and the art museums of Springfield—as many stops as one week end would permit.

The smaller New England museums have a color all their own. Rich as they are in works of art, they do not pretend to be treasure houses. Their aim is not to own art but to show it. Primarily educational institutions, they do not attempt to direct taste; they exemplify it. For the most part they are privately endowed, and thus independent of state subsidy and popular favor. As disinterested members of the republic of arts and letters, they direct themselves solely to that solid social class so important in New England—the college educated. They are as characteristic of the region, and as admirable, as the New England schoolteacher, and just as different one from another.

Of those I visited, the Wadsworth Athenaeum is the most sumptuous. Its collection is the most important, its establishment the most urbane. The entrance hall with its Baroque marble fountain was expressly designed for elegant functions and civic displays (the ball held there in 1935 with paper costumes and decorations by Tchelitchew is still remembered) and its Avery Memorial Theatre was inaugurated by the first performance of the Stein-Thomson opera, *Four Saints in Three Acts.*

The principal part of the Athenaeum's collection is known to New York from having been shown here last year at Knoedler. It contains one of the best Rembrandts in America—a portrait of a young man, hard, handsome, determined, and secretive; one of the most striking of all the Zurbarans—a *Saint Serapion* in the white robes of his order, fainting in chains; and a beautiful panel by Goya of two women conversing, in Goya's cheerful, early, tapestry-cartoon style. The museum is rich in Baroque and Mannerist paintings which A. Everett Austin, its late director, was one of the first to esteem. There is a surprising number of first-rate pictures by comparatively unknown names. Contemporary pictures are numerous and well selected and include the collection of *Ballets Russes* designs, both scene and costume drawings, which Serge Lifar inherited from Diaghilev. Everything connected with the institution is marked by a taste that is at once lively, distinguished, bold, and up-to-date.

The Smith College Art Museum is more sober in its installation as befits the working museum of a college. Its collection properly avoids a general panorama of art—so easily available in the large municipal museums—and specializes in the French nineteenth century, on the sound scholastic ground that this is the source of all contemporary painting. Its two most spectacular pictures, an enormous unfinished Courbet and an even larger unfinished Degas, were certainly acquired for the light that such uncompleted work throws upon a painter's methods. The Courbet—*La Toilette de la Mariée*—is an elaborate and spacious composition, six by eight feet, with some fourteen figures. It is painted with a flat brutality that is surprising in so highly skilled an artist, and almost makes one suspect that the picture had been carried further than Courbet left it, by a less skillful hand. The Degas—*La Fille de Jephté*—is more convincing. It has rich warm color, a biblical setting, and numerous figures in every degree of finish. Since the picture has not been completely pulled together, the subject and action are by no means clear. It nevertheless remains one of the most interesting of Degas' early works and the largest and most elaborate he attempted in the Beaux Arts Competition style.

Along with these are Bonnards, Vuillards, a fine Cézanne and one of the best of Seurat's preparatory paintings for *La Grande Jatte*. There is a sketch for a *Maréchal de France* by Hyacinthe Rigaud; an unexpected gray and green landscape, by Gauguin, of the Paris suburbs; a spectacular imaginary view of the pyramids by Hubert Robert; an equally romantic *Nocturne* by Eugène Berman, and one of the finest of the 1920 Cubist Picassos. The French part of the collection is supplemented by works from other schools, such as examples of American and English eighteenth-century portraiture and English Romantic landscape. As one can see from the works cited, the pictures at Smith have been chosen with an eye to their value as typical or instructive examples.

The Worcester Museum is a handsome building in a classical Renaissance style. It is richer and older than Smith; its scope is also wider, proposing, as it does, to present in outline the history of art. From the main entrance hall with its Roman mosaic pavement from Antioch, one moves through a series of ascending galleries, from Egyptian and Mesopotamian, through Classical and Oriental, and so on to the work of today. The early exhibits, though not numerous, are carefully selected—a wonderful Catalan twelfth-century altar frontal, for example, a particularly fine Cambodian head, and enchanting Persian miniatures. Later painting has a more copious display. There is Piero di Cosimo's delightful *Discovery of Honey,* with all the fauns and satyrs banging pans to drive the swarm of bees, and Bacchus and Silenus thoroughly enjoying the excursion. There is a *Diane de Poitiers,* perhaps by Clouet, pale and bejeweled at her dressing table. There is a *Bergamask Captain* in black on gray by Moroni, and two wonderfully cheerful Hogarths of a Mr. and Mrs. William James, so pleased at being painted.

The museum is rich in early American portraits (fine ones by Christian Gulligher whom I have not encountered elsewhere) and in nineteenth- and twentieth-century Americans. One remembers especially a beautiful Whistler of a woman in a short, fur-trimmed jacket, painted in easy, liquid brushwork; and a late Monet of *Waterloo Bridge* in a purple dusk. The moderns include a well-known boy in profile by Picasso, a monumental standing nymph by Braque, and the various styles of Abstraction. The whole establishment has something of the municipal dignity of New York's Metropolitan.

Springfield has two art museums. One, the George Walker Vincent Smith, has little intellectual distinction. Erected in 1895 to house the Smith collection, it is a dusty period piece, a monument to a taste now gone out of fashion. Amidst its armor, porcelains, bronzes, Renaissance-style furniture and other *objets d'art,* hangs an oil depicting Mr. Smith himself, his kindly face set off by a snowy two-pronged beard, and his severe wife, surrounded by their treasures. Some of the Oriental objects he amassed may be very fine—I am not capable of judging—but the statuary and pictures are without exception dreadful: polychrome marble busts of Germanic warrior maidens, Canova's *Queen Elizabeth* with ruff in bronze, and justly forgotten American and Italian genre painters of the eighties in massive gilded frames. One wonders how any collector in that vigorous age of painting could have guessed so consistently wrong.

The real museum in Springfield, the Museum of Fine Arts, is quite another matter. It is a fairly recent institution. The building itself dates from the thirties and is in the severe, uncorniced Rooseveltian post-office style of the time. The collection is perhaps less rich than Worcester's but has a remarkable piquancy. One remembers, for example, a fourteenth-century Catalonian *Fall of Simon Magus* by Domingo Valls, in which the presumptuous ecclesiastic is ridden in his fall by three black spiky demons, while saints and gentlemen watch from below in scandalized disapproval. Here is the only Guardi portrait I have seen—a young boy in the blue and gold brocaded uniform of a Venetian military academy.

There is an exceptional Courbet of *M. Nodler the Younger,* an intense and unpleasant student-intellectual; and a quite wonderful unfinished painting of a vivid young man with palette and mahlstick—obviously a self-portrait by a painter—but here attributed to Delacroix as a study for a portrait of the Baron von Schwiter. The nineteenth- and twentieth-century American group includes among its examples of *trompe l'oeil* John Haberle's torn *20 Dollar Bill*—the most deceiving I have seen. There is a fine collection of American Primitives, the grandest being the fantastic and enormous nine-by-thirteen foot *Historical Monument to the American Republic* by Erastus Salisbury Field. This, a mad architect's dream, presents an edifice with ten pinnacled and becolumned marble towers, linked at the top by ribbons of girders, adorned with numbered bas-reliefs and statues illustrative of events in American history, the whole surrounded by trees, lawns, and visitors in 1880 costumes, and enlivened by inscriptions in biblical, prophetic, and topical vein. Pictures such as these, perhaps not the most valuable but each in its way unique, and chosen with an odd and humorous acumen, are what give the Springfield Museum its particular distinction. And museums such as this, not the richest, perhaps, but numerous and well directed, are what most clearly reflect New England's intelligent preoccupation with art and culture.

# *Carnegie International*

IN ADDITION to its celebrated international exhibition of contemporary art, the Carnegie Institute of Pittsburgh is holding this year a retrospective exhibit chosen from previous Internationals. The Institute itself is a large, formal, somber building in one of the Renaissance styles. Properly speaking, it is not an art museum but a library to which has been added a concert hall, a museum of natural history and a fine arts department. The warm and old-fashioned decoration of its lobbies, its pleasantly informal attendants, its displays of mounted dinosaurs and habitat groups, its cafeteria full of young people with books and parents with children, make it like some well-ordered, easygoing municipal club. It has none of the stiffness of a museum on guard over its treasures. Its small collection of old masters—not now on view—is an accidental, unforeseen accretion. Carnegie was not a collector of antiquities; he was an educator who planned to expose Pittsburgh to contemporary art and to encourage contemporary painting. His Institute was probably the first of the modern museums.

From the beginning the Institute's exhibitions were international and had enormous—even international—prestige. The first, of 1896, showed Degas; showed and bought Whistler, Sisley, Sargent, Mary Cassatt and Boudin. Raffaëlli, a minor French Impressionist, won second prize, the jury being the art committee of the Institute. For some years thereafter, the jury was made up of ten painters elected by the contributing artists and the shows became somewhat more conventional. Except for Eakins, who won a prize in 1907, no top-class names occur in any of these first years' awards, and prizes usually went either to second-string practitioners of Manet's style of brushwork or to second-string Impressionists.

In 1922, under the new director, Homer Saint-Gaudens, the system was revamped. The prize jury, consisting of painters and occasionally of museum people, was appointed by the director himself, who also, as now, selected the contributing artists and, most probably, the particular works. Contrary to what one would expect, perhaps because a certain amount of log rolling was eliminated, shows under Saint-Gaudens became more up to date. They reflected the advanced styles of representational painting one associates with the Whitney Museum of those years, and many of the more famous European Moderns—Derain, Matisse, Picasso, Bonnard, and Dali —were honored with awards. Since 1950, with the appointment of Gordon Washburn as director, the character of the exhibition has again changed to become now almost entirely non-objective.

The ninety-five canvases of the retrospective summarize this progress. Only a part of the pictures were actually exhibited here before; the rest are stand-ins, though by the proper painters, for works now unavailable. There has been, naturally, a certain amount of editing. The more unfortunate side of the nineties is represented by only two examples—a horrid *Little Red Riding Hood* by George Frederick Watts and *American Beauties,* a girl dreaming over roses in the worst calendar style. Two large pictures by Abbey and Lucien Simon, which won prizes in 1901 and 1905 and now hang in the Institute's library wing, have not been brought into the exhibition rooms. Like so much fashionable painting of the time, they no longer seem very serious. To compensate, there are many fine Impressionists.

Beginning with 1922, the selection is more varied. Almost every famous name is represented and with particularly well-chosen works. There are three beautiful Bonnards, three characteristic Picassos of which two are the finest possible (one a synthetic Cubist and one a pink), a 1926 *Odalisque* by Matisse in stained-glass color, some top-notch examples of German Expressionism, one of the best of Klee and one of the best of Rouault. There is an extraordinary work—a full-length portrait of an elegant black man in full dress uniform, *The Haitian Ambassador,* by Kees Van Dongen, a fine painter one unfortunately never sees. It is a brilliant and praiseworthy show.

The contemporary international exhibition is even more brilliant, but more difficult to remember. It is enormous—almost five hundred pieces, of which one-fourth are sculpture—and very successful as to sales. Even this early—ten days after the opening—there are ninety-four gold stars. The pictures themselves are almost all large and showy. Very little of the work is representational (though the gold stars occur in much higher proportion on these) and almost none of it offers a conventionally recognizable image. Every imaginable device of pattern, texture, color, or even association is employed for attracting the attention: A black-and-white checkerboard, distorted as if by superposed lenses, dazzles the eyes until it seems to move. Adjoining it is another picture, which actually does move because the spots are motorized. One canvas offers a regular sequence of the ten digits cut from newsprint and half covered with gray paint, and another, considerably less sophisticated, presents a donkey out of Picasso, braying at three Van Gogh sunflowers. All the prize-winners are non-objective, although the fourth prize, *Changeable Weather,* by Vieira da Silva, might conceivably represent a street in a drizzle of rain. The first and third prizes, each of more than thirty-six square feet, are respectively a low bas-relief in gray-painted papier mâché, and a loosely attached assemblage of strips of wood veneer.

The non-objective style is clearly international; thirty-one nations are represented. The Japanese seem most consistently successful in it

—not surprising since calligraphy and texture are the fundamentals of their Classical painting. The Italians have fine paint quality, the Spaniards show frequently a brutal brush stroke, while the Americans seem fond of the incontinent drooling characteristic of Hans Hofmann's studio school; the French try out a little of everything. Amid such exuberance, even the brashest representational painting in the show—John Bratby's huge bright *Interior with Monopoly Board* with child and nude and higgledy-piggledy furnishings—seems tender and restrained, and the more conservative painting of Wyeth and Kokoschka looks distinctly out of place.

The character of an exhibition like this—since the world is full of painters and all sorts of pictures—depends principally on who does the choosing. A group of painters picking out a show is likely to favor their immediate associates. However catholic their professional judgment may be and however strict their respect for technical excellence, practicing artists will not actively champion work very different from their own. A group of collectors will be more liberal. They will tend to sponsor all the various kinds of work they would themselves collect. Their selection, based on estimations of a picture's permanent value, will be inclusive though conservative. An exhibition director, on the other hand, has neither the painter's narrow professional loyalties nor the collector's interest in solid acquisitions. He wishes above all to make an effective show. And the high brilliance and visibility of the present International characterizes it at once as a director's choice. A director of Burlington House once explained to me, and only half jokingly, that the aims of a Modern painter should be two—to out-shout any other picture in an exhibition and to look well by electric light. A director of the present Institute, no more interested than the Royal Academy in permanent collection, cannot but have a similar point of view. His aim is brilliance and he will accept anything that is newsworthy.

In the present case he has been enormously successful. The exhibit presents the most extreme the world has to offer in the way of high visibility and novelty. But visibility and novelty are now standard academic qualities. The techniques of high visibility form today the principal study in even the most conservative art schools. And—since the serious painting of the last eighty years has for the most part been in revolt against conservative standards—students are taught as academic and undisputed dogma that art can exist only as a progression from one novelty to the next. Nevertheless, visibility emptied of all content, even the pornographic, and novelty that no longer quite surprises, can make a diverting show but not a memorable one. One wonders how long any of these pictures will hold our affection. The Zuloagas with their sloe-eyed Spanish gypsies, and the Sorollas with their incomparably brilliant brushwork—still hanging in the library entrance hall—so visible and shocking forty years ago, today attract hardly any notice at all.

# *The Smithsonian*

THE SMITHSONIAN INSTITUTION of Washington, with its hodgepodge of historical mementos and ingenious gadgets, of natural history, ethnology and art collections in this and last century's taste, has always been one of my favorite museums. The Smithsonian is a huge enterprise. Its buildings on the Mall include the Museums of Arts and Industries, of Aviation, and of Natural History, as well as two museums of fine arts—the Freer and the semi-independent National Gallery. Elsewhere in Washington it runs a zoo. In Cambridge it possesses an astronomical observatory, and in the Canal Zone, a tropical island. The Institution itself is the most important of our learned societies. It conducts scientific research, sends out expeditions to the lesser-known parts of the earth, and acts as a free distribution center for international exchange of scientific publications. Its astonishing collections of oddities, art, and marvels are only somewhat accidental accretions on what is basically a scientific foundation.

The story of the Institution's origin is like the plot of a Victorian novel. James Smithson, the founder, was English, a gentleman, and illegitimate. His father, a commoner who rose to become Knight of the Garter and Duke of Northumberland, was the husband of his mother's cousin. With this family drama in the background, it is not surprising that Smithson's mother gave birth to him in France. And it was under her name of Macie that he entered Oxford. The fortune he inherited came entirely from his mother's side of the family. Smithson's great passion was chemistry; he became a fellow of the Royal Society, friend of Cavendish and Arago, spent most of his time abroad—apparently he had no love for English society—and died in Genoa in 1829. He never married. His considerable fortune he left to his nephew with the casual proviso that if the nephew died without children—which he did—the money was to go to the United States to found "an establishment for the increase & diffusion of Knowledge among men." The bequest, amounting to more than half a million dollars, was accepted by Congress only after much hesitation. The first plan—to use the bequest to found a university—was abandoned in favor of a foundation for scientific research and publication, complete with library and museum, and having all the financial and political advantages of being a ward of the federal government.

The Board of Regents' first meeting was in 1846. Only two years later the Smithsonian issued its famous *Ancient Monuments of the Mississippi Valley,* the first of its publications; was already providing grants and apparatus for outside scientific work; and was carrying on its own scientific investigations. A number of these, in geology, weather, fisheries, Indian ethnology, and so on, proved important enough to the government to warrant special subsidy and have even given rise to special government bureaus. Congress began to supply funds for certain of its programs, and private benefactors began to add their donations of art as well as money to Smithson's original bequest. Since our government contains no department of fine arts, it was decided in court that the Smithsonian —which already possessed a small collection of paintings from the Smithson inheritance—was also a National Gallery of Art and the natural custodian of all bequests of art intended to form part of a national collection.

In 1855, the first of the Smithsonian buildings was erected, to house, among other things, Smithson's collection of minerals. It is a wonderful Romanesque pile (or Norman or Lombard or Twelfth Century, as you will) by the New York architect, James Renwick, Jr. With its dark red stone and nine towers, no two alike, it is, to my way of thinking, the finest piece of architecture in all Washington. In the early eighties the Arts and Industries Building was erected, in the exposition style of the time, to receive objects inherited from the Philadelphia Centennial. The Freer and the National Galleries on the same side of the Mall, designed to hold the art collections left to the nation by Freer, Mellon, Widener and Kress, are too well known to speak of here. The Natural History Building across the way is somewhat earlier than these. Built in standard 1910 "Classical," it contains, in addition to its exhibits of natural history and ethnology, a collection of art both instructive and entertaining, but so much out of fashion today that the National Gallery will have nothing of it.

These pictures belong principally to the official American School of fifty years ago. Some, like Thomas Moran's huge mountain landscape, or Childe Hassam's charming adaptations of Impressionism, stand up very well. But for the most part, time has not treated kindly these ladies at spinets and sweet Arab maidens in their elaborate frames. Even more dated are the story-telling pictures—George de Forest Brush's clammy-skinned Indians, lined up like Disney characters in a canoe, precariously hoping to spear a moose; or Puvis de Chavannes' mawkish idea of what went on in Fra Angelico's studio, which he was pleased to call *Inspiration Chrétienne*.

The two specialties of the Natural History collection are the works of Abott Thayer and Albert P. Ryder (twenty-three pictures of the one and fifteen of the other), which serve to illustrate the two extremes of late nineteenth-century painting in America. Thayer, something of a New England Tiepolo, was a fine draftsman, with clean color and carefully considered tone relations, direct and unsentimental in his work. But his subject matter, limited to depiction of a sort of noble purity (calm-faced mothers and college girls got up as angels) is as impersonal as the engraving on a bank note, and the result is as cold as a fish. Ryder, much more famous today, was not cold at all. He was a wild Romantic with as subject all the Romantic commonplaces from *Flying Dutchmen* to *Dancing Dryads* and *Pegasus (departing)*. But, to judge from the pictures here, he could neither paint nor draw. Apparently his knowledge of painting methods was also faulty, for the pictures are so crevassed and darkened that it is impossible to tell what their color might have been. Despite the few somewhat better Ryders to be seen elsewhere, I suspect that it is entirely because of its poetic aspirations that his work has acquired the importance it is given today.

All this makes one regret that the Smithsonian's unique collection of Catlin's Indian pictures is not on view; they are incomparably more interesting. George Catlin was a self-taught painter from Pennsylvania, originally a lawyer, who spent from 1830 to 1836 in Indian country, doing portraits of Indians and landscapes of the plains. He considered his pictures not as art, but as documentation, as a plea against the deprecations the Indians were suffering, and he exhibited them, charging admission, in all the Eastern cities and later in London and Paris. It was the first Wild West Show, with Indian costumes and weapons, more than five hundred paintings of Indians, and live Indians brought along to do war whoops and dances. After some years of great success, Catlin fell into debt. A fellow American bought the pictures and shipped them home to Philadelphia. It is this collection, recovered from a cellar, which the Smithsonian possesses almost entirely—four hundred twenty-two of the five hundred seventeen paintings listed in Catlin's 1840 exhibition catalogue.

However great its value as ethnology, the collection is even more fascinating as painting. Catlin worked fast. He must have done three or four pictures a day, always—except in landscape—on the same size canvas and with the simplest of palettes: blue, black, white, vermilion, ochre, and brown. He would first sketch in the subject, usually a portrait head or a single standing figure, laying it in in brown on an already prepared neutral-tinted ground, and then proceed to finish the head and as much of the figure and background as there was time for. Few sitters were allowed more than one pose. He probably painted sitting, sometimes even on the ground. The somewhat disturbing enlargement of the lower limbs of some of the figures looks like distortions caused by looking up at the model from below, distortions which remained uncorrected because of the rush of work to be done. On the other hand, the fresh directness of the painting, and much of its power to communicate, come from the rapidity and spontaneity of its execution. The one picture with "studio finish" is much inferior to the others. The landscapes, fresh as they sometimes are in color, do not have the portraits' precise characterization and seem to have been painted from memory. But the portraits and figures are like nothing else I know. The calm beauty and intense presence of these faces are not to be found in the work of any of the other painters of Indians. Let us hope that, as part of the modernization program the Natural History Museum is now enjoying, the collection will eventually be put on show along with the handsome new Indian habitat groups. They are the one evidence we have that the "Noble Savage" of the eighteenth-century philosophers was not entirely a fiction.

One of the Modernizations soon to be on view is a marvelous new swimming whale, a life-size model suspended overhead in the suavest of S-curve dives, almost too graceful to be thought of as a fellow mammal. My other particular favorite here (the unicycle with rider seated inside the wheel, the transparent matron, the

Wright brothers' airplane, and Washington's false teeth are in the Arts and Industries Building) is the display of money from the Island of Yap—immense stone disks too heavy to be moved, a thoroughly stable monetary system whose basis of credit (like the early Spartans') was too ponderous ever to be stolen, lost, or squandered.

From the constant crowd of visitors here, I suspect that everyone else finds the rich confusion of these exhibits as fascinating as I do. And however imposing the Smithsonian itself is as a scientific institution, its buildings are certainly the most delightful place I know to spend a rainy day.

# *The Middle West—Cleveland, Toledo, Detroit, St. Louis, Kansas City, Chicago*

## CLEVELAND

THE CLEVELAND MUSEUM sits back in a splendid park to the east of town. It has a large and open dignity, not at all municipal, but rather like some princely residence temporarily vacated, and in its sober opulence bears a family resemblance to the Frick in New York. The original building, erected in 1916, has just recently been remodeled—doubled in size by the skillful addition of a wing in the shape of a hollow square—and provided with all the latest in museum equipment from overhead daylight lighting and exhibition halls with movable partitions, to batteries of television cameras which act as electronic museum guards. The building is luxurious but in no way forbidding or oppressive, and the collection it houses is rich in masterpieces.

The institution had its origins in the eighties when three donors, each independent of the others, left funds to found a museum. Nothing was done until 1913 when the three funds were combined and the museum was incorporated with a princely endowment. Cleveland, like Chicago, has a long history of picture collecting. Such collections have a way of ending in the local museum, and as soon as a Cleveland museum was established, collections began to pour in. The first of these was donated by Mrs. Liberty Holden in 1914, two years before there was a building to house it. It consisted of a group of Italian primitives assembled in the seventies and eighties, long in advance of contemporary taste, by James Jackson Jarves, who had also formed the celebrated Jarves collection now at Yale. The bequest was quickly followed by others, both collections and funds. Since the directors knew in advance what the private collections contained and what pictures they would eventually inherit, they were able to use the funds to buy what would not be given. As a result, Cleveland's coverage is astonishingly thorough, with good examples of almost everything esteemed today, especially in European painting.

The European collection is, indeed, too rich even to begin enumerating. The *Adoration* by Filippino Lippi is probably the finest Lippi in the country, and Tintoretto's *Baptism of Christ* is one of the most lyrical of the painter's mature works outside of Venice. There is a glowing *Adoration of the Magi* by Titian, complex in composition, unusual in scale, and apparently unfinished; one of the best Bassanos—of Lazarus, dog, and rich man's supper table; two celebrated Grecos; fine Tiepolos, Rubens, and Van Dycks; good English portraits; one of the most dramatic Turners—*The Burning of the Houses of Parliament*—with flames reflected in the Thames and dark foreground boats crowded with spectators; and a living, speaking portrait by Goya of an architect friend, done on a black priming instead of Goya's more usual brick red.

French painting is particularly well presented. Along with top examples by all the predictable eighteenth- and nineteenth-century names there are also surprisingly good pictures by nineteenth-century painters now rarely exhibited—such as a sea fight between Greek and Turkish vessels by Eugène Isabey, as beautiful in the Romantic style as a Delacroix; or the recently cleaned *Coast Near Villerville* by Daubigny which now appears with color as bright as Monet's; or the *Reclining Nude* by Couture, with so temptingly painted a bottom as to require the protection of a pane of glass. As for the more Modern masters, there are charming Renoirs and Van Goghs; the *Frieze of Dancers* by Degas, one of the very best; the most beautiful Berthe Morisot—of a young lady in white seated on the grass of a spring pasture; a celebrated Cézanne, a celebrated Lautrec, and Gauguins, Matisses and Douanier Rousseaus, along with some well-known early Picassos.

American painting goes from colonial work down to the present. There is one of the best Eakins—a portrait-landscape of two oarsmen in a racing shell; good Innesses and Chases and exceptional examples of painting of this century from Sloan and Kroll to Graves and Marin. In comparison, the more Abstract of the American contemporaries seem relatively neglected, although the museum is beginning to acquire some representative examples. When I was there, a monster retrospective of Feininger was being held, and the museum's well-known May show is devoted entirely to contemporary Cleveland artists.

One of Cleveland's great specialties is its collection of medieval bronzes, carvings, textiles, and jewelry, whose most costly and barbaric items are the portable gold altar and jeweled crosses acquired from the Guelph Treasure of the Royal House of Brunswick. The museum is particularly rich in such bibelots and smaller sculptures—pre-Columbian, East Indian and Chinese—and Roman portrait heads; the period rooms contain some of the best and rarest of eighteenth-century furniture. In one of these hangs, as a luxurious joke, two eighteenth-century tapestries. One is a French *Chinoiserie* depicting, in the Boucher style, a Chinese fair. The other is authentic Chinese, showing a children's party in honor of the birthday of a small prince—so urbane, civilized, and well behaved that the French tapestry by comparison seems almost *nouveau riche*.

What most distinguishes the Cleveland Museum is the absence of the second rate from its collections. This general high level of quality is partially due to the fortunate circumstance of its founding and growth. But there is also the equally fortunate circumstance that Cleveland has never been forced, as have so many museums, to exhibit inherited collections as unit memorials to the donors. This freedom was established by its second president, Mr. J. H. Wade, who with modesty and foresight refused to allow his own donations of works of art to appear on permanent exhibit in galleries labeled with his name. Since then the directors have consistently reserved the right to edit the collections the museum accepts and divide them as they see fit. This, added to Cleveland's extraordinary endowment —second in funds only to the Metropolitan—makes it today, despite its relative youth, one of the great museums of America.

## TOLEDO

The Toledo Museum of Art is built in the Greek Classical style much employed for public buildings of the first quarter of our century. Opened in 1912 and enlarged in 1926, it was further extended in 1933 by the addition of two lateral wings. One of these houses the Peristyle, Toledo's municipal concert hall—a semi-circular Greco-Roman theater.

Handsome as the building is, it enjoys little of its neighbor Cleveland's palatial grandeur. It has rather the solid but slightly shopworn air of a university building. And that, in a way, is what it is —a municipal institution engaged in art education for all ages, with courses ranging from drawing and painting, ceramics and art teaching (with college credit), to classes in home decoration and in appreciation of Modern art and music. When I was there, a special educational exhibit of excellent Modern pictures, taken from the museum's own collection and borrowed from elsewhere, was being hung to illustrate the theme *What Is Modern Art?* More than Cleveland, Toledo is actively interested in contemporary Abstract art, and the American non-objectives receive more emphasis here than elsewhere in the Middle West.

Unlike Cleveland, Toledo is primarily a single donor's museum, with one principal benefactor and three or four inherited collections—a monument to the taste and generosity of a very few persons. Founded in 1901 and principally endowed by Edward Drummond Libbey, a manufacturer of glass, its nucleus was Mr. Libbey's own collection of old masters, and of ancient and modern glass. The other principal inheritance was the collection of paintings donated by the museum's second president, Mr. Arthur J. Secor.

Mr. Libbey's personal acquisitions, as inherited by the museum, included some fine pictures, such as—to mention only a few—a head of an old man by Tiepolo; a Velasquez, masterful in color, of a smiling cavalier with gloved hand and wine glass; an unexpected Cranach of *Martin Luther and his Friends;* a self-portrait by Rembrandt as a young man in a plumed hat; an excellent Holbein of *Catherine Howard;* a Turner of a Venice lagoon in clean, clear blues; and a convincing and unflattering self-portrait by Reynolds. Along with the better paintings there were formerly also a number of French and Dutch nineteenth-century landscapes, today out of fashion, only the best of which are kept on view. Since Mr. Libbey's death in 1925, this original collection has been extensively increased with purchases made with funds he left for that purpose.

The Secor collection, shown together in a memorial gallery, is much less good. It consists chiefly of English eighteenth-century portraits and salon landscapes in fashion in the eighties by painters like Diaz, Daubigny, Israels, Mauve, Millet, and the later Corot—

a plethora of peasants, oak trees, cows, and sheep. It nevertheless contains the one first-class Theodore Rousseau I have seen, of a line of birches in an evening light.

The American collection of eighteenth- and nineteenth-century painting is incomparably more varied and important. It is based on a few pictures donated by Mrs. Florence Scott Libbey, but consists in the main of works bought with money she bequeathed. One remembers particularly a masterpiece by Thomas Cole—*The Architect's Dream*—in which a miniature figure of the architect reposes on a divan made up of huge folios atop an enormous architectural capital of a pseudo-classical order, while the landscape behind him displays a river, with a fleet of galleys, gardens and fountains, and monstrous buildings in all the styles from early Egyptian to American Protestant Gothic. Mrs. Libbey's bequest, along with a smaller collection of twentieth-century pictures (including a fine Wyeth) bought with the bequest of Miss Elizabeth Mau, a Toledo school teacher, and the museum's more recent contemporary acquisitions, provide a complete display of American painting from colonial Primitives to William Baziotes.

What with the original inheritance and the pictures subsequently acquired, the museum is now in possession not only of some very valuable and beautiful pictures, but some very unusual ones as well. I think of a wonderful Courbet of a plump girl in profile before a trellis of flowers; an imaginary landscape by Patinir with blue rocky peaks and towns and castles and in the foreground, as an afterthought, a tiny Paris as a shepherd with his goddesses; a very Neo-Classical David—*The Oath of the Horatii*—as formalized as a ballet and as gaudily theatrical as Ben Hur; Clouet's *Elizabeth of Valois;* a Ter Borch *Music Lesson;* two Grecos, one a fine *Annunciation* and the other a *Gethsemane* in the painter's most flamelike Baroque manner and exceptionally acid color. Among the odd and more unusual, there is a melodramatic *Destruction of Tyre* with black tidal waves of glassy water in a livid light by the English

Romantic John Martin; and a full-length portrait by William Rothenstein of the English painter of fans, Charles Condor, dressed in a tubular overcoat of *fin de siècle* elegance and caught in the act of languidly closing a door.

Among the moderns there is a small, pink-period Picasso *Head of a Woman,* as well as his famous and sentimental picture from 1904 of a woman caressing a crow. There are good examples of all the standard Impressionist and Post-Impressionist masters—Degas, Cézanne, Gauguin, Renoir and Matisse, and a very beautiful Bonnard landscape called *Europa and the Bull.* In all, Toledo's coverage of American and European art is fully representative and contains some remarkable pictures. If the museum seems on the whole less impressive than some of the others in the region, it is not on account of the absence of fine examples from its collection, but on account of the presence of some second-rate ones. Such a situation is generally remedied in the long run by the directors, simply by eliminating the duller pictures and stocking up with interesting ones. That is what is being done here, and rapidly. But the situation itself is an all too common one and inevitably arises when the inheritances a museum receives are in the form of indivisible collections.

As a postscript, and as a curious proof of how the eye changes with time, let me quote from the museum's out-of-print catalogue of 1939. Its description of a Soutine, entitled *Color Arrangement* —which Toledo no longer owns—sounds very contemporary:

> Dynamic swirls, broad strokes of closely related colors . . . attain fine balance in a composition surcharged with motion. Semblance of form is subjected to rhythmic pattern of color and texture.

The identical Soutine—judging from the dimensions and photograph in the Toledo catalogue—is now on display in the Museum of Modern Art, and bears as title what now it quite unmistakably represents—*Dead Fowl.*

## DETROIT

The Detroit Institute of Arts occupies a sumptuous and comfortable building completed in 1927 in a simplified Renaissance style. The interior, with its halls and courts and suites of paneled rooms, each furnished in the period of the paintings and objects it displays, has a rich baronial air not out of keeping with the great barons of industry who are its benefactors. The institution itself is older than the present building. It began back in the eighties and was fathered by a newspaper.

In 1883, the Detroit *Evening News* organized for the city a large loan exhibition of pictures. It was such a success that the paper, in the person of its advertising manager, Mr. William Brearley, was able to raise funds to build a permanent museum which opened in 1889. However, Detroit had no art collection for the building to contain, and the institution was in danger of becoming a combination of art school and exhibit hall for contemporary shows. Mr. James Scripps, editor and publisher of the *Evening News,* found this unsatisfactory and undertook to furnish the museum with pictures. He had already had some experience as an art collector and believed that the old masters had more permanent value than the contemporary works of Diaz, Mauve, Meissonier, and Bougereau, so dear to the collectors of the eighties. Besides, the old masters were a great deal less expensive than famous living painters. (One remembers the story of the visitor to Meissonier's studio being shown the painter's collection of old masters—a Rembrandt, a Titian, and so on. "Why," says the visitor, "do I not see one of your own works?" "Oh," says Meissonier, "I can't afford it.") So, with values and prices in mind, Mr. Scripps set out to acquire old masters, principally among the minor Dutch, and in 1889, when the museum opened, he was able to endow it with seventy pictures. Other well-to-do Detroiters followed his example, sometimes with less acumen, and the galleries were presently filled with all sorts of

Turkish and Persian bric-a-brac, plaster casts, and natural history specimens. As one of the trustees complained in 1910, the museum made it a rule to accept all gifts in order to avoid hurting the feelings of well-intentioned givers.

In 1919, all this was changed. Under Michigan law, the art museum, since it was not a municipal institution, could not use municipal funds. Therefore a new city charter was adopted, providing for a city art commission which would build a new museum and administer it as a department of the city government. At the same time the older private museum corporation was retained as a sustaining society. Under this dual leadership, partly old Detroit society, partly municipal, the present museum building was erected, and Dr. William Valentiner was engaged as director.

Dr. Valentiner, a highly cultivated German, brought to Detroit the idea, new in museum practice, of culture-history. According to this idea each cultural period has a spiritual unity. Works of art shown for themselves alone, as separate *objets de vertu,* are interesting only to the specialist. They can be understood by a broader public only when shown in their proper historical context, under which conditions the spirit of their cultural period becomes apparent. Thus, each gallery of a museum should as much as possible present—with its paintings, sculpture, and decoration all drawn from the same period—a unit illustration to a particular chapter of the history of culture.

On this educational basis the new museum was conceived. Since no attempt was made to carry it to extremes, it works very well, with European galleries from Gothic to eighteenth century ranged in the right wing, and in the left, a series of American rooms with art from the seventeenth century until today. The display of Classical and Oriental art is less extensive, difficult perhaps to display under such a system. But there is a large and comprehensive collection of modern painting, both European and American.

The Institute's own endowment is small. Its collection derives chiefly from private benefactors who have always, except during depression years, supplied the museum with funds to buy the works it needed and contributed pictures from their own collections. The European collection, valuable as it is, tends to be perhaps a little dull. Its solid values and particular emphasis on the great names in Flemish, Dutch, and Italian painting, reflect the conservative taste of the rich benefactors as well as the Central European formation of Dr. Valentiner himself. There are, nevertheless, any number of pictures too lively or important to be indiscriminately dismissed as "old masters." One remembers—to mention only a very few—a Tintoretto ceiling; a portrait by Titian of a *Man with a Flute;* a superb Bronzino of *Eleonora da Toledo and her Son, Don Garcia;* two charming portraits by Barocci of the *Prince of Urbino* as a serious and melancholy child; Rogier van der Weyden of *Saint Jerome in the Desert,* bald, in a flaming vermilion robe, doctoring the paw of an amiable and somewhat heraldic lion; Pieter Breugel the Elder's *Wedding Dance* with hundreds of capering figures; a delightful scene by Zoffany from *Love in a Village,* a popular eighteenth-century English comic opera; a fine Hogarth portrait of a pretty and silly woman; and Van Dyck's *Marchesa Spinola* of a very distinguished one.

On the other hand, the American collection got together under the curatorship of Mr. E. P. Richardson, now the Institute's director, is one of the best in the country. I was particularly struck by a Negro head by Copley—a sketch for one of the sailors in *Watson and the Shark*—which seems to combine the skill of Velasquez with the humanity of Watteau. There are good Homers, Eakins, an almost Impressionist Eastman Johnson of berry pickers in a cranberry bog; a *Trappers' Return* by Bingham—two hunters in a canoe on a misty river with their pile of gear and pet raccoon—of which the Metropolitan has another version; Whistler's *Nocturne in Black and Gold; the Falling Rocket*—an almost non-objective spattering of yellow confetti on a dark night sky—the very picture from which the Ruskin-Whistler defamation suit arose. There are good Sargents, Mary Cassatts, Gari Melchers and so on down to Franklin Watkins, Kuniyoshi and Georgia O'Keeffe. The collection of American furniture and decorative objects in this wing is completed by what I have not seen elsewhere—a display of the church furnishings of eighteenth-century Canada.

The section devoted to more recent European painting is equally complete. There is one of the best of the early Courbets—an outdoor sleeping nude called *Midday Dream,* and one of the best Degas in the *Dancers in the Green Room.* There is a famous Van Gogh self-portrait in a straw hat, and one of the most sun-drenched Monets—a woman with sunshade beside a bed of gladioli. The German Expressionists, whom Dr. Valentiner was one of the first to esteem, are given an extensive showing with probably the best examples of their work to be found in American collections. I remember particularly a *View of Jerusalem* by Kokoschka, whom I believe the finest of the living landscape painters working in the Post-Impressionist style. The non-objective wing of contemporary painting is also amply represented.

One is reminded how up-to-date Detroit has always been by the presence here of Diego Rivera's enormous mural which a few years ago brought the Institute into such lively notice. Made to decorate the building's interior court with scenes from the industrial life of Detroit, it jumped into the news when someone thought to find in one of its panels—a doctor and nurse innoculating a child—a parody of the Nativity. The joke today seems less pointed, and the mural itself, with its dusty fresco tonality and jerky variations in scale, seems strained and thin. It is, nonetheless, a notable example of yesterday's most advanced official art, and one is glad to see it here, if only for historical and educational reasons.

Just as the Cleveland Museum has the character of a treasure house, and Toledo a memorial to its principal contributors, the Detroit Institute of Arts is essentially an educational and scholarly foundation. Publishing *The Art Quarterly*—an international magazine of art scholarship—and busy compiling for its Archives of American Art a complete documentary record of American painting from colonial Primitives to the latest on 57th Street, with its solid European coverage and its beautiful and complete survey of American art, it represents the best to be found in the Middle West of conservative and respectable scholarship and taste.

## ST. LOUIS

The City Art Museum of St. Louis occupies a Palace of Art building left over from the Exposition of 1903, in style a restrained World's Fair Roman. The columned entrance portico—flanked by seated marble figures of Painting and Sculpture, and crowned by six standing figures symbolizing art in its various periods, from Classical to Modern—leads to a large central hall situated between the two lateral wings containing the exposition galleries. The central hall, with its grandiose proportions, has the impressive emptiness of a courthouse lobby or railroad station waiting room, and quite dwarfs the pieces of sculpture and Hubert Robert panels which adorn it. The galleries themselves are better scaled for exposition purposes and contain, along with the museum's collection of paintings and art objects, a suite of American and European period rooms, a medieval cloister court and chapel, and a gallery, which I found particularly fascinating, of old St. Louis, with early scenes and portraits, paintings of Indians, engravings of steamboats, and river navigation charts.

The museum has a history older than the building it occupies. It all began in 1879 as part of the Fine Arts department of St. Louis' Washington University and ran on university funds. In 1906, the collection was separated from the university and transferred to the present building, which had been donated to the city by the exposition company. And the institution, now as a city museum, was provided by the city with funds for its support, deriving from a city property tax, and put under the governorship of a self-perpetuating municipal board of control. This city tax, now amounting to some $330,000 annually, is still the St. Louis museum's principal support and the chief source of its collection.

One wonders what the original university collection could have contained. By present standards it must have been quite inferior, for little from it still remains on show. Actually, in the present catalogue, only one object acquired before 1915—an engraving after Lebrun—is thought worth mentioning. And the complete list of acquisitions before 1920 is limited to an Umbrian *Madonna and Child;* two Dutch pictures—a Van Goyen skating scene and an excellent Ter Borch; four Impressionist works—a Monet, a Manet, a Sisley, and a Pissarro; a Gilbert Stuart sketch and three other unimportant American paintings; an Italian oak cassone; a medieval iron coffer; a sixteenth-century steel breastplate; two Persian platters; two Chinese bronze mirrors; a Japanese No mask; five European engravings; and a piece of gold and red Italian brocade.

Thus the St. Louis collection is of comparatively recent origin, and has had less support from private bequest than Cleveland, Toledo or Detroit. The greater part of its possesions seems to have been purchased by the museum itself with its own funds. It nevertheless possesses today a considerable and representative collection of European and American painting—fifty of the best pieces were shown at Wildenstein in New York in November, 1958—along with a not unimportant collection of the decorative, Classical, and Oriental arts, including a celebrated group of early Chinese bronzes.

The most important pictures in the collection are perhaps the early Tintoretto of *Minerva Pursuing Venus,* the Rembrandt *Portrait of a Young Man,* and the Holbein of *Lady Guldeford* which, despite its masterful execution, is nevertheless hard and metallic in its detailed drawing, and garish in color, as well as being of a particularly uninteresting sitter. There is an expressive late Titian *Ecco Homo* with a benevolent Pilate and a mischievous boy; a characteristically dramatic landscape by Magnasco; a charming picture by Mme. Vigée-Lebrun of her young brother; a self-portrait of the young Goya; a sturdy and economical still life by Zubaran;

and an arresting Mannerist painting of an unquiet and sensitive Florentine gentleman with, as background, a cascade of moss-green drapery.

Among the later pictures, there is a beautiful *Girl with Mandolin* and a *Beach at Etretat,* both by Corot; a fine small study by Delacroix for his *Barque of Dante;* and this along with all the great Impressionist names, including a delightful portrait study by Lautrec.

Among the modern Europeans there are Picassos (a particularly fine pink nude of 1907); Gris (an exceptional 1917 Cubist checkerboard); and Braques (including a still life of 1944, surprisingly good for that period of his work which I have always considered inferior); and a wonderful *Marseilles Harbor* by Kokoschka. For more unusual items, there is a large early Derain of soldiers in a suburban dance hall; and a large, cheerful, and colorful Chagall of Adam and Eve and the serpent, more in the Italian Futurist style of dislocated triangles than anything else of his I know.

The American school is well presented—early portraits by Copley, Earl and Gulligher; a number of good Binghams; an Arcadian landscape by Cole; a beautiful Kensett of the *Upper Missouri* in light clear colors; with Homer, Harnett, Chase, and other nineteenth-century names well in evidence. The later Americans I was not able to see; their exhibition halls have been taken over for a show of 15 of the younger painters from France—loud, large, and non-objective, and, I am afraid, all too familiar.

The city of St. Louis itself boasts of some notable private collections—of the Pulitzers, the Weils, and others. Indeed, when I was there a large show of locally owned Picassos was just ending at the Artists' Guild and the collection of German Expressionist painting of Mr. and Mrs. Morton May, perhaps the largest in the country, was on show at the library of the St. Louis University. Many of these pictures, if one can judge from the history of other Midwestern collections, will eventually end in the museum here. Most certainly it can find place for them. However well St. Louis has managed on its relatively small budget, it still has nothing like the wealth of pictures and art objects donated, so often, by private collectors to other museums of the region, and on the whole is less rich in outstanding examples than in famous names.

## KANSAS CITY

The Kansas City museum is a spacious, well-designed building in a Neo-Greek style. With the exception of Cleveland, it is the newest and most up-to-date museum of the region—opened to the public, while still unfinished, in 1933 and completed in 1949. Unlike the City Museum of St. Louis, it has no municipal dependence. Its full name—The Nelson Gallery of Art and Atkins Museum—records its origins. And its position as one of the finest art museums in America derives entirely from the generosity and foresight of private individuals.

William Rockhill Nelson, who died in 1915, the museum's founder and chief benefactor, had probably never in his life bought an original picture. Owner and publisher of the *Kansas City Star,* his experience in the arts was limited to collecting books and, after the fashion of a somewhat earlier generation, to acquiring copies of the old masters. But as a cultivated and public-spirited man, he believed that his city should have an art museum, and set up in his will a trust fund for buying works of art. The fund's principal asset consisted of the *Kansas City Star*. This, put up to auction and bought by its own staff, brought $11,000,000. Other members of Nelson's family, and his lawyer as well, left money and land to provide a building. There already existed in Kansas City another trust for the same purpose, left by Mary Atkins in 1911. The two trusts were put together by their trustees. And with the resulting foundation, the present museum was built and furnished with collections.

Nelson, as a newspaperman, had little confidence in the stability of changing city administrators and made elaborate provisions to protect his museum from local vagaries. He arranged to have at the head of the trust three state university presidents—of Missouri, Kansas, and Oklahoma—presumably on the assumption that one president might be venal, but all three could not possibly be. The three presidents were empowered to appoint three acting trustees, the institution's actual heads, who were charged with administering the estate, buying works of art, and appointing the museum staff.

The formation of the collection began in 1930. For assistance and advice in the European field, the trustees engaged Harold Parsons, whose great reputation for taste and reliability allowed him to follow the unheard-of double calling of picture dealer and museum man. The adviser in Oriental art was Langdon Warner, the great Harvard authority. Later, Paul Gardner became director. Laurence Sickman, who spent many years in China acquiring objects for the museum's celebrated Oriental collection, succeeded Gardner and is the museum's present director.

If one had money, the depression years were wonderful for buying works of art. And with both money and expert advice, the Kansas City museum acquired some marvelous stuff. Let me list a few of the most striking items:

A portrait head in diorite, noble and sensitive, of a Babylonian king, probably Hammurabi the law giver; an Egyptian Fifth Dynasty portrait statue in wood of a crown administrator, worried and withdrawn, not at all unlike the executive head of some contemporary intellectual publishing concern; two astonishing seventeen-inch Hellenistic terra cottas of boxers—one a barbarian with a beard and loincloth, the other Greek, nude as was the Greek fashion, and with the heavy long straight hair that is still a characteristic haircut of young Greeks today—in my opinion two of the finest Hellenistic pieces in the world. There are some excellent Roman heads, including both a convincing portrait of Hadrian and a reasonably unidealized Antinous; a Christian Coptic candlestick sporting a very unchristian Venus with her make-up kit; along with some of the best examples of medieval sculpture.

As for paintings: a delightful Florentine panel of a timid and retiring *Madonna of Humility* by Lorenzo Monaco; a *Virgin and Child* at home in a Flemish interior on a summer day, by Petrus Christus; a speaking portrait of a young man in a plumed hat by Bronzino; an aristocrat, reserved and watchful in black, by Titian; a large important Veronese of *Christ and the Centurion,* with fourteen figures in the painter's most mature and sumptuous style; a sulky and sultry young *John the Baptist* by Caravaggio; *The Three Graces* by Cranach, perverse and stylish in their well-groomed nudity; one of the best of all the Greco single figures—a *Trinitarian Monk*—self-possessed and insolent; one of the best of the Goya portraits—a commanding and withdrawn *Don Ignacio Omulryan y Rourera,* Minister for the Colonies under Charles VII, an Irishman, one would suppose, from his name and reddish hair; a late Rembrandt of a youth; a portrait by David of a brooding Creole boy; an Ingres of a young sculptor, romantic and suspicious; and one of the late and most impressive of Cézanne's versions of *Mte. Ste. Victoire.*

The American collection has exceptional examples of all the eighteenth-century portraitists—Copley, Earl, Stuart, and all the rest; Raphaelle Peale's celebrated *After the Bath*—a work which depicts an oil painting of a bather, presumably nude, over which has been hung, for modesty, a draped sheet rendered in the most convincing *trompe l'oeil;* a whole room of portraits and genre pictures by George Caleb Bingham, mid-century painter of the local region; and the finest Catlin in existence, of a fierce little *Indian Boy* got up in war dress.

The Oriental collection is said to be one of the very best in the country. It was apparently assembled at a time when the interest in the field was less general than now, and the entire collection cost the museum less than their Rembrandt and Hobbema together. The group of Chinese sculpture contains some extreme rarities (such as the sixth-century bas-relief from the cave chapel of Lungmen, Honan) and is dramatically lighted and displayed, as is indeed everything else. The collections of Chinese painting and pottery are full of extraordinary examples in all the periods, and so is the Japanese collection.

The Indian collection contains examples of sculpture from all periods, of Hindu painting, and the interior of a seventeenth-century temple. And the young standing Buddha from sixth-century Siam, in meditation and with melancholy downcast head, strikes me as one of the most touching pieces I have seen. The museum has another display I find particularly engaging—a collection of cages, race tracks, tongs, and whips, the complete paraphernalia for the Chinese sport of cricket racing.

One can see from this small listing what extraordinary masterpieces Kansas City has succeeded in assembling. When it came to acquiring contemporary work, however, there was a difficulty. Nelson had drawn up his will very shortly after the Armory Exhibition of 1913 when Modern Art first appeared in America. He must have shared his friend Theodore Roosevelt's suspicion of it, for in his will he had directed that no work should be bought with his bequest before the artist had been dead for thirty years. A museum, nonetheless, needs contemporary pictures. These were supplied partly by private donation of modern works, but chiefly by the formation in 1934 of a society, The Friends of Art, which has now some thousand members whose contributions provide for the purchase of contemporary pictures. Thus the museum has now a good and growing collection of contemporary European painting and an even more complete American one.

The museum organizes loan exhibitions and puts on an annual show of works—which it offers for sale—of painters and sculptors from the eight midwestern states. As an educational institution operating in connection with the University of Missouri, it is also empowered to give a master's degree in museum curatorship. It is the only memorial museum I have ever thoroughly approved of. For it is a memorial not to the donor's power of acquisition and foibles of taste, but to his warmhearted civic pride and intelligent foresight. Looking at his portrait here by William Merritt Chase, one realizes that Mr. Nelson must have been a very fine man.

## CHICAGO

Of all the museums of the Middle West, the Chicago Art Institute is by far the most splendid. Along with the New York Metropolitan, the Museum of Fine Arts in Boston, and the National Gallery in Washington, it is one of the four great museums of our country. It is also one of the country's largest and most reputable art schools. And, as a matter of record, it was as an art school that it began.

A year after the Civil War, a group of Chicago art students organized a school for themselves. It must have had enormous vitality and fanatical support, for it endured through the Chicago fire which destroyed its equipment, and through the panic of 1879 which did away with its entire assets. In 1882 it was re-established under the name of the Art Institute of Chicago, this time as both an art school and a museum. An impressive building in the Romanesque style of the architect Richardson was built to house it. And though it still operated principally as an art school, it began to acquire a collection, consisting for the most part of plaster casts from the antique for the use of drawing classes. At the end of Chicago's Columbian Exposition of 1893, another much more suitable building became available—a large, well-built Italian Renaissance palace made for the fair to house the World's Congress of Religions. The Institute took it over (the original building on Michigan Avenue now houses the Chicago Club), and at that point began its serious career as a museum.

In this transformation, the famous Mrs. Potter Palmer was a leading spirit. Beautiful, rich, and cultivated, she was the brightest star of Chicago's social life. There still hangs in the Institute a dashing portrait of her, by Zorn, in white with pearls and wand

and diadem, as fairy queen for a costume ball. Her own family had French connections. She knew Europe well and followed European fashions so closely that already in the seventies she was buying Barbizon pictures and by the eighties had gone in for Impressionism. Having been president of the *Lady Manageresses* of the Exposition, she was particularly interested in the new museum and supported it with money, time, and donations of pictures. Her lead was followed by her son who was the principal contributor to the Institute's collection of old-master prints.

Chicago was then full of enthusiastic collectors. There were the Martin Ryersons who, with exceptional taste, were collecting even in the early 1900's Impressionist pictures and Italian Primitives, and who contributed to the Institute, among other things, the great six-panel Giovani di Paolo. There was the McCormick-Deering family, friends of Sargent, who had a castle in Spain and who collected Spanish Primitives. There was Arthur Jerome Eddy, the lawyer, who went to Europe in 1895, where he was painted by Whistler and modeled by Rodin, who bought the Institute's Kandinskys from the Armory Show and who in 1914 wrote the first book in America on Modern Art. There was Henry Field, brother of Marshall Field, who gave the Institute its then most popular picture—Jules Breton's *Song of the Lark.* (The most popular picture today is Renoir's *Two Little Circus Girls.*) There were the Frederic Bartletts who collected Lautrec, Van Gogh, Cézanne and donated Seurat's chef d'oeuvre, *La Grande Jatte;* and Mrs. Lewis Coburn who lived in a hotel room and specialized in Impressionists and Post-Impressionists, which she kept in closets and under the bed. There were the Buckinghams, two maiden ladies and their brother Clarence, who bought Chinese bronzes, Japanese prints, Medieval sculpture and old masterprints; and the Charles Worcesters, who as friends of the director, Robert Harshe, bought under his direction whatever the Institute needed, from High Renaissance to Vuillard; and Joseph Winterbotham, a man of impeccable taste, who furnished the Institute with, among other things, Lautrec's

*In the Cirque Fernando: The Ringmaster* and Chagall's *Rabbi of Vitebsk;* the Spragues who bought from the Havermeyers the great Greco *Assumption* which Mary Cassatt had found for them in Spain and which the Havermeyers let go because it was too big for their house; the Kimballs, Brewsters, Mungers, Wallers, and many more, all vying to supply the institution with pictures.

The resulting collections are too rich even to attempt to describe. I will pass over the Oriental collection which contains among other things some eight thousand Japanese prints, and only speak in passing of the Thorne collection of miniature rooms—sixty-seven American and European period interiors, microscopically complete even to the landscape outside the windows—and go on to the paintings. The Institute is particularly rich in German and Flemish works. To mention only a few outstanding examples, there is the famous *Adam and Eve* of Cranach; a Jerome Bosch *Garden of Paradise* with fantastic grotto and fountain, as fine as anything outside the Prado; a beautiful portrait of a *Man with a Pink* by Quentin Massys; and a young girl looking through an open half-door, undoubtedly one of the best Rembrandts in America.

As for Italian work, there is an exceptional Tintoretto of *Venus and Mars,* with Cupid, serving girl, and the Graces in attendance; a Florentine burgher by Ghirlandaio, probably the best portrait of his in the country; and four extraordinary scenes from *Jerusalem Delivered* by Giovanni Domenico Tiepolo, I would imagine, rather than by his father. The most popular picture here by far is a large and handsome work of Caravaggio's school—a furious Mars, his arm upraised to thrash a naked and blindfolded Cupid, flat on the ground and howling. Among the Spanish pictures there is a most unusual and beautiful Velasquez of a Moorish boy-servant with downcast head in white turban, waiting, pitcher in hand, behind the counter of an inn; and six small Goyas which recount in comic-book sequence how young Fray Pedro got the best of the bandit Maragato.

French painting begins with a sixteenth-century portrait of a man with a glove by Corneille de Lyon which might be mistaken for Degas. There is, in *St. John on Patmos,* what many museums claim and few possess, a real Poussin; and *The White Tablecloth* is the best Chardin still life I have ever seen. Nineteenth-century painting has complete representation and includes admirable pictures by painters like Fromentin and Millet, today generally considered negligible.

It is in Impressionism and Post-Impressionism, however, that the Institute astonishes. Its collection is every bit as fine as the *Jeu de Paume's* in Paris, perhaps finer. Here is the best of Mary Cassatt —a woman in striped dress bathing a child; and the best of Berthe Morisot—a woman in silvery gray at her toilet table. The Manets are numerous—eleven or twelve of them—but to my taste too much in his Velasquez-inspired salon style. On the other hand, there is a room of admirable Degas, twelve of them including the almost Japanese *Millinery Shop* and the vivid double portraits of *Uncle and Niece* and *Mme. Lisle and Mme. Loubens.* There is a room of Renoirs; a room of Monets—which is, however, only half of what the Institute has; the best and biggest Lautrecs; some of the best Matisses; seven or eight Cézannes and six astonishing Gauguins including the portrait of Marie Derrien with, as background, the Cézanne still life Gauguin owned. One must not forget Douanier Rousseau's jungle *Cascade,* or the most famous item of all, Seurat's *Sunday Afternoon on the Island of La Grande Jatte.* The twentieth-century School of Paris is equally well represented with Braques, Picassos, Brancusis, Soutines, Derains, and the rest.

American eighteenth- and nineteenth-century painting is completely displayed, often with better works than one had thought their painters capable of—as, for example, the *Third Beach, Newport* by Kensett, the *Corn Husking Bee* by Eastman Johnson, the luminous blue *Gloucester* of Twatchman, and the dark and brooding *Mrs. Charles Gifford Dyer* by Sargent. The Institute's collection of Innesses I did not see; some of the galleries were then being rehung. But there were other things to compensate, including a sardonically detailed plucked chicken by Harnett, every pimple there, entitled *For Sunday's Dinner.*

As for twentieth-century American, the collection contains all the most publicized pictures of our time from Grant Wood's *American Gothic,* Peter Blume's *The Rock,* Jack Levine's courtroom scene, *The Trial,* and Albright's sinister still life of a hand-held bonquet before an embossed tin door, down to all the "name" Non-Objective painters of today.

Curiously, all through this trip I have been hearing complaints from museum people about the Non-Objectives. In Detroit I was told that their painting grounds and pigments were for the most part either of bad quality or badly handled, that the pictures were rapidly deteriorating and would be impossible to restore. At Kansas City, the complaint was rather of their size: that the cost for keeping an average-size picture on the wall—figuring the expenses of guards, museum maintenance and so on—ran to about three hundred dollars a year. And that a large Non-Objective work occupies the space of three or four more concentrated works. And in Chicago I was told that the local young private collectors were stocking up on the Non-Objectives to the neglect of the sort of pictures the Institute would prefer to inherit.

Be that as it may, the fact remains that in Chicago, after a lull of many years, an enormous amount of private collecting is being done, perhaps more than anywhere else in the country, at all price levels and in all the ranges of taste. And, if past models are followed, all these collections will eventually be available to the Institute. There is a new director, Mr. John Maxon. The Institute is being refurbished, repainted, relighted, and rehung, and pictures, good pictures, hidden away for years are being given wall space. The Art Institute has for a long time been one of America's most important museums. It is now on the way to becoming one of our most exciting ones.

# *Mrs. Kennedy's White House*

IT HAS recently been my great pleasure to see the White House and its new redecoration. The building itself turns out to be much larger than one would imagine from the photographs. The large central section, rebuilt under Monroe after the fire of 1814, is rendered even more impressive by the two wings of offices added by Theodore Roosevelt, while the tall north and south porticos, built in the eighteen twenties in the Classical Revival style, confer on the whole the unmistakable air of a palace. Precisely this palatial dignity is what Mrs. John F. Kennedy's new decoration of the public rooms is designed to underline. She has been remarkably successful.

This is not the first time the White House has been redecorated, usually in one of the advanced styles of the period—in the modern, so to speak, of the day. President Monroe redid the reconstructed mansion in the latest thing in Empire furniture and gilt bronze ornaments and vermeille flat wear, all from Paris—not from England or from here. To buy from the British who had just burned the city would have been inconceivable, American workmanship was not that good or up-to-date, while Empire itself was the modern idiom of Monroe's day, more advanced even than the Greek Revival style his friend and neighbor Jefferson had helped invent. President and Mrs. Lincoln in their time did the place over in the latest Victorian. Under McKinley the prevailing style was Eastlake-Victorian relieved by pieces of *Art Nouveau.* Theodore Roosevelt hung the walls of the dining room with mounted animal heads—a royal hunting lodge fashion much in favor in his time. And the Steinway grand piano, designed apparently by Franklin D. Roosevelt himself, still stands in the great East Ball Room, an epitome of the corniceless streamlined style of the twenties with a frieze of gold-leaf figures in the manner of Rockwell Kent, and for legs, three massive wing-furled eagles like plump and somnolent owls. Under Truman the whole interior was rebuilt and redone in the style of a refined and luxurious middle-western country club; and through Eisenhower, that is what essentially it remained.

To confer formality and dignity on such an interior was Mrs. Kennedy's admirable intention. For this, the modern decorative style of today, however right it might be for a League of Nations or a United Nations building and however constantly its previous forms have been used in White House decoration in the past, will not do at all. Our government has been in existence much too long. One would as soon think of redoing the Houses of Parliament in glass and stainless steel. Today's modern style is too much lacking in reverence. One remembers in this connection the Byzantine sculptors who, when carving a particularly precious piece of ivory, would sometimes emphasize its preciousness by working not in their own contemporary style, but in the more imposing idiom of Pre-Christian Greece. For the purpose of defining a palace today, something of the same sort of stylistic retrogression is required, a style with richer historical associations than today's modern could supply. Let us for convenience call it First Settler Legacy.

This is a purely American, or Colonial, not a European, style. It has as stylistic basis the type of furnishings used in a particular region by the first prosperous settlers. Its character varies with the region. In Boston it is English Eighteenth Century. In New York its less pretentious form is the Dutch farm house, its grander form, after New York City's city hall, is late eighteenth-century French. In the deep South it is Victorian (although Atlanta uses late Eighteenth and early Nineteenth Century English because it believes that *Gone with the Wind* is factually true). Southern California inclines to Spanish Mission, though San Francisco is principally General Grant and Denver is Edwardian and *Art Nouveau*. All this is proper and understandable. These are the heirlooms, the kind of furniture one's ancestors in these places might have possessed. I would, nevertheless, like to insist that though First Settler

Legacy as a style makes use of antique pieces, it is nonetheless a strictly contemporary idiom based on contemporary ideas, fashions and materials, and aims to present a historical background for contemporary living rather than give any accurate presentation of the past, and in fact has very little to do with what the past was actually like.

The proper stylistic model of White House decoration is obviously the American version of Directoire-Empire known as Federal, the style of the early part of the nineteenth century when our national expansion first began and when, under Monroe, the first of the reconstructed White House's furniture was acquired. Unfortunately, when Mrs. Kennedy first took charge, very few of the historic pieces remained; apparently almost nothing, in fact, dating earlier than 1902. Heretofore, White House furniture has always been considered more or less the personal property of the presidents, who, likely as not, at the ends of their terms would move out with whatever they wanted. One of Mrs. Kennedy's first accomplishments was to see that this custom was changed. A bill has now been passed by which the White House furnishings become a permanent collection, administered by the Smithsonian Institution and exhibited or stored by them when not in use. France possesses a similar arrangement in its *Guardemeuble Nationale,* a store house for all the art and furniture belonging to the French Government, whose business it is, among other things, to provide French embassies and consulates abroad with fine furniture, tapestries and paintings.

The acquisition of historic pieces for the White House has been entrusted to a fine arts committee composed of curators and directors of the principal American museums. But the selection of material and discriminating taste displayed in its arrangement can be attributed to Mrs. Kennedy herself. Particularly successful is the diplomats' large oval reception room with its wonderful scenic wallpaper printed in Alsace, as well as the Red Sitting Room with its Empire furniture and gilt bronzes and double tiers of pictures in bright gold frames. It is all, in fact, handsome and distinguished and surprisingly opulent considering that American Federal is not the most sumptuous of the decorative styles. Louis XVI, English Palladian, and even certain aspects of Victorian offer far greater opportunities for ostentation and display. Mrs. Kennedy has had to face as well the difficulty that good American pieces of the period are hard to come by. Federal America was still a provincial country, and despite a few exceptions, workmanship here was far inferior to that abroad. It is not surprising to find that most of the fine pieces in the White House came from France.

Of the White House pictures themselves, unfortunately little can be said. Only three of them now on exhibit have anything more than an antiquarian historical interest. One is a fine romantic portrait of President Tyler by the Paris-trained Bostonian George P. Healey, dated 1858. The others are a picture of Angelica Van Buren by Henry Innman, and a full-length Washington, a gift of Equador, painted by Luis Cardena of whom nothing seems to be known. The large standing Washington, supposedly a Gilbert Stuart original, is crudely executed and vastly inferior to other works by Stuart in the National Gallery. And the two Cézannes, gifts of the late Charles Loeser, both fine enough but very green, are not at all enhanced by the green brocade on which they hang. Their *repoussé* gold-leaf frames, smacking of 1912, are all too out of place in the Federal setting. As for the early nineteenth-century landscapes, none can bear comparison with the Coles and Kensetts and Bierstadts elsewhere in Washington. This, however, is a minor and, in the present setup, a temporary flaw. What has been accomplished in so little time is very impressive, and the work is by no means completed. From the constant crowds of visitors of all ages, one realizes that the White House has become a national shrine. In previous administrations there were not as many visitors. Nor is this surprising. Under Mrs. Kennedy the White House is beginning to acquire an air of being not so much the residence as the palace of our presidents.

# *The Barnes Collection*

In 1951, at the age of seventy-nine, Dr. Alfred C. Barnes, Philadelphia philanthropist and art collector, drove through a red light and was killed. He left behind him, in the Barnes Foundation, one of the world's largest and most celebrated collections of pictures. It was also one of the least accessible. No catalogue existed; no picture from it was ever loaned and no photograph allowed to be reproduced. Relatively few persons had seen it—only the small body of students matriculated in the foundation's courses of art appreciation, a scattering of the doctor's personal friends and picture dealers, and such guests and applicants as were acceptable to his despotic and unpredictable whim. Getting in was very difficult. One wrote a letter of request, which often remained unanswered and as often was refused. Emily Genauer, the art critic, was turned down apparently because she had telephoned to the foundation's unlisted number. Jacques Lipchitz, the sculptor, was not let in although the foundation contained many and most important examples of his work. James A. Michener, refused under his real identity when a college student, got in by pretending to be a steelworker from Pittsburgh.

This last is not astonishing. Barnes was a self-made man, and however difficult he may have been with those of wealth or position, he always professed sympathy for what he called "plain people." Born of very poor parents in a Philadelphia slum, he had helped pay his way through medical school by playing semi-professional baseball. And when he became rich from the invention of argyrol, he retained a warm and somewhat Whitmanesque regard for ball players, firemen, and Negro spiritual singers. He had known the painters John Sloan and William Glackens in school;

he himself had even tried to paint. As soon as he could afford it, he began to collect pictures, and called on Glackens for advice. That was in 1910 or 1911. Glackens was devoted to the French Post-Impressionists and particularly to Renoir, and had no use for the conservative pictures Barnes was then acquiring. He introduced him to a more contemporary style of painting, with such effect that in 1912 Barnes dispatched him to Paris with $20,000 in his pocket to spend on modern works. Glackens bought him a small Renoir—a *Girl Reading,* the Van Gogh *Postman* and other Impressionist and Post-Impressionist works. Barnes must have liked them immensely, for six months later he was himself in Paris buying his own. By the middle twenties his taste and acumen as a collector in the modern field had become so celebrated that in 1923 his latest seventy-five acquisitions were given a special exhibition by Paul Guillaume in his Paris gallery. The show aroused such general interest that it was immediately brought over to be exhibited by particular request at the Philadelphia Academy of Art.

Barnes' other major interest was popular education, an interest probably awakened by the influence of his life-long friend, the philosopher and teacher John Dewey, whose theories of education have had such a profound—and I suspect unfortunate—effect on the American teaching system. Barnes believed passionately in the possibility of bringing culture and philosophy within the reach of the ordinary working man, and began by offering classes in psychology to the workmen in his factory. He also hung a selection of his modern pictures on the walls of the plant. And in 1922, for the express purpose of teaching art and art appreciation according to the guided group-discussion methods advocated by Dewey, he established and endowed the Barnes Foundation, and donated to it his constantly growing picture collection.

In 1922, when the foundation was begun, modern painting was some forty years less familiar than it is today, and examples of it correspondingly more difficult to evaluate. Barnes himself chose his pictures, I believe, the way all great collectors do. He bought pictures and kept them around, and those that died on the wall he traded for others. Nevertheless, he thought that he had found, in a variant of Clive Bell's "significant form," a sure and objective method of art criticism. It was roughly this: the subject matter of the picture as well as the work's poetic content were to be disregarded. One was to look only at the plastic (or formal) means employed. These formal elements he considered to be color (which included light), line and space. Barnes maintained that the value of a work of art could be accurately determined, first, by the expressivity achieved by each of these elements taken separately, and then by the unity of effort arrived at by their combined use. He was also convinced that the best way to teach the appreciation of great painting was to put a student in front of a masterpiece and teach him to evaluate it by this system of analysis. He even believed that in this way students could be taught to paint original works.

Consequently, the foundation was staffed with instructors trained in Barnes' method of criticism, and endowed with the best possible examples of modern painting to serve as material for analysis. The courses were entirely philosophical and verbal—no practice or training in drawing or painting was permitted within the institution. Especially was it forbidden to make copies of the pictures on display. Students were accepted on grounds of their general suitability and Dr. Barnes' approval. No previous knowledge of art or art history was required. There was no tuition.

The school has now been in operation for more than thirty-five years. Despite the doctor's great and constant generosity in grants and traveling fellowships, the results have been disappointing. A few art instructors and writers on esthetics have been turned out, but as far as I know there has not been a single painter of any value—a record that could have been predicted for a school of art education based entirely on the ritual admiration of masterpieces.

Although he established the art gallery as a functional part of his teaching system, Barnes did not, I believe, at first intend to render it as inaccessible to the general public as it soon became.

The foundation's original trust indenture provided that the collection would be open to the public three days a week, the times and conditions to be regulated at the discretion of the board of trustees. That was in 1922. In 1923, the much-heralded exposition of Barnes' new Paris acquisitions was held at the Philadelphia Academy. The results were deplorable. The pictures—particularly, it seems, those of Soutine—were more than Philadelphia could take. There was an immediate and outraged uproar. Barnes was deeply hurt and vociferously furious with public, critics, and museums alike. And when the foundation was inaugurated the following year, Philadelphia found that he had taken his revenge. He had invoked the discretionary clause in the charter; the public was excluded and the collection was accessible only by particular invitation.

The policy was continued after Barnes' death, although I believe that latterly any qualified person, on writing a letter, has been received. Now, however, the interdict is over. The State of Pennsylvania, after a series of long and difficult legal maneuvers, has succeeded in establishing the principle that a charitable, tax-free institution like the Barnes Foundation falls under the supervisionary jurisdiction of the state's attorney general, and must be administered for the public benefit. And it is announced that, after a date not yet named in the near future, the public up to the number of two hundred will be admitted to the foundation two days of the week, that on the other days the gallery will be open to art students and instructors by arrangement, and that to facilitate requests, the foundation's telephone number will henceforth be listed. Whether the foundation's school continues under this public invasion is a matter for the directors to decide. It probably will go on, since if the classes cease, the foundation's income falls under the attorney general's supervision.

The collection, which I have recently had the privilege to see, is every bit as extraordinary as one was led to believe. There are about a thousand pictures—some two hundred Renoirs; a hundred

Cézannes; seventy or eighty Matisses; twenty to thirty Picassos, all of the early and most valuable periods; fifteen or twenty Douanier Rousseaus; one of the largest and finest Seurats, depicting his studio with model; numerous Van Goghs, Soutines, Modiglianis, Pascins, along with examples of all the rest of the School of Paris—even including one not-too-important Derain, a painter whom Barnes, I am told, particularly disliked. There is a collection of locks and keys, of Negro sculpture, of Early American furniture, tapestries after designs by Picasso and Rouault, a Matisse mural, a large group of Flemish and Italian painting including a fine Tintoretto and a Titian portrait of a man with a little boy; the man, wearing a short beard and a troubled expression, resembles for all the world the present director of the School of American Ballet.

The monetary value of all this, at present market prices, is fantastic. Of course, it would be quite impossible, even if one wished, to sell a collection like this outright. Such massive unloading would destroy the market. Nevertheless, I am told by Mr. Georges Keller, of the Carstairs Gallery and formerly of the Bignou, who acted as Dr. Barnes' agent in purchasing a greater part of the work, that if, little by little, buyers could be found, the collection would bring in something between three hundred and five hundred million dollars. None of the collection is insured. Dr. Barnes maintained, quite sensibly, that a work of art is irreplaceable, and that insuring it serves no purpose.

The building that houses the pictures stands back in wooded grounds—a large, pleasant, open, rectangular, limestone structure in a simplified French Renaissance style, resembling more a fine private mansion than a picture gallery. In fact the pictures are hung as in a private house, with little attempt at placement according to painter, date, or school. Each frame carries the painter's name but gives no indication of the picture's title—all very much in keeping with Dr. Barnes' attitude toward subject matter. His particular favorites among the painters were Matisse, Renoir, and Cézanne, all of whose various manners are here exhaustively exemplified.

There are even pictures that the doctor himself recognized as faulty, but which he acquired to show his classes how badly the greatest artists could sometimes paint. There is, for example, a girl by Renoir with a clumsily drawn forearm, and a well-known Cézanne figure piece—four men bathers and Mte. Ste. Victoire in the background—which, with its poison-green grass and stickily painted bodies, could scarcely appear more laboriously uninspired. On the other hand, there are two portraits of Mme. Cézanne, one with a single glove and one in a hat, as noble and direct as Titians; the most successful of the large figure compositions; the famous *Boy with Skull;* the even more famous large finished version of *The Card Players;* together with the finest imaginable collection of still lifes and landscapes, the greater part unknown to the public, even, I believe, in photographs.

As for Renoir, beginning with four large decorative panels of nudes in a somewhat pre-Impressionist mural style, there is a complete and extraordinary presentation of all his periods, from the pictures painted on the Marne as a very young man, down to the best, fat, pink ladies of his latter years I have yet seen. The Matisses, on the other hand, I found disappointing. And the famous mural, with its flat, monochrome figures silhouetted like cutouts in three contiguous lunettes, is so slight and economical as to leave almost no impression at all. The Matisses of the Cone collection in Baltimore seem to me much finer. But then, in Baltimore Matisse is not placed cheek by jowl with such much greater masters.

It is almost useless to go on with the enumeration—of the two splendid large Picassos, one a blue period of a boy and man in juggler costume, the other a pink, of a nude girl, child and goat; the disquieting Pascin of a young woman and little boy; the numerous, important and delicious Rousseaus; the curious Degas of two reclining nudes and a pair of standing legs, looking almost as if cut out from a larger canvas; the Lautrec portraits and the tiny Daumier of a painter at his easel, certainly Daumier himself; the Bonnard of a woman at a red-covered table addressing invitations.

Particularly gratifying are the numerous Glackens. Glackens has always been rated an inferior imitator of Renoir. But here, where the two painters can be so beautifully compared, it becomes clear that the charge is unfounded. Glackens' brushwork, it is true, derives from Renoir's, but there the likeness ends. Glackens' bright color contrasts resemble not at all Renoir's quiet and meditative harmonies. And Glackens' brash exuberance of sentiment and subject bears no likeness to Renoir's mellow cheerfulness and restrained good manners. From the wonderful examples shown here —the charming self-portrait as a young man, the race track on a summer day, the New England bathing scene—it becames evident that Glackens is not a French imitator, but a straightforward American painter and one of the very best.

It is, in sum, a magnificent collection. True, it dates a little. With no Surrealism and little Abstract work, and including as it does a few names now out of style, it evokes more than a little the esthetic climate of the twenties—of *The Dial* and *Broom* and *Vanity Fair*. According to the articles of incorporation, neither the hanging nor the composition of the collection can ever be changed. As time goes on it will probably appear more and more a period piece. I do not think it will suffer from it. With so few inferior pieces and such a superabundance of outstanding ones, it should weather even the most radical changes of taste.

Dr. Barnes was a controversial figure. Whatever can be said about him, of his implacable resentments toward those he considered his adversaries, or his great generosity toward his intimates and friends, he was after all, as his collection demonstrates, a princely type with a prince's taste for the best in painting. And despite his affirmed devotion to a somewhat arid theory of artistic formalism, the emphasis he placed in his collection on the human values in painting is evidence enough of his humanity. Neither he nor his collection will soon be forgotten.

NOTE: Background material for this article is taken from *Art and Argyrol* by William Schack (Thomas Yoseloff, 1960).

# SHOWS IN PARIS

## SPRING 1958

In Paris, walking is still a delight. The large, easy perspectives of bridges, trees, and fountains bathe in a palpable, submarine air, as visible as water in an aquarium. It is not surprising that a city so pleasant to the eye should be addicted to the visible arts. If in New York everyone talks music, in Paris everyone talks painting. And in the fresh spring weather, along with lilacs and chestnuts, bloom everywhere bright posters announcing new exhibitions.

The show of a hundred paintings by Modigliani at the Charpentier Gallery is the most popular. Only at our Modern Museum have I seen such crowds. The entry is four hundred francs, almost a dollar, and one must wait in line. To my taste the pictures are not worth the scramble. One hundred is too many. They lack variety. Almost all are portraits, full face, with the same linear stylization, the necks and head elongated, the eyeballs black as if the pupils were enormously enlarged, the mouths pursed. In spite of their great tenderness and their airy and nacreous color, the Modiglianis have something of the slick and uniform professionalism of the café painting of *Montparnasse*. One thinks of him as a more sensitive and warmer-hearted Kisling. Modigliani's great popularity is easy to understand: his subject matter is humanly touching, his pictures are impossible to mistake, and the Romantic irregularity of his life would seem to confirm his genius. We may soon expect a movie.

Universally and justly admired are the one hundred forty-three paintings and objects loaned by the Japanese Government to the *Musée Nationale de l'Art Moderne* and illustrating the history of Japanese art from prehistoric times till now. Both in the quality of the works and in the manner of their display, this is the finest exhibition of Eastern art it has ever been my pleasure to see.

If one is accustomed to think of Japanese art as the most stylized of the Oriental traditions, the show is a great surprise. The thirteenth-century pieces are particularly expressive and varied—two statues, for example, of celestial messengers, a young man and an old woman, whose attitudes announce without possibility of mistake their characters, their caste and the quality of news they bring; or the wonderful scrolls of animals playing at being people, of the many nerve-racking discomforts of Hell, of prophets, monks and poets undergoing their adventures in dramatic or civilized landscapes. But there is also the more spontaneous painting of the Zen monks and masters of the next two centuries; an extraordinary panel by the fifteenth-century Hasegawa Tohaku of pines progressively disappearing behind a curtain of rain; and a seventeenth-century screen describing the arrival of a Portuguese ship, the landing of its commander accompanied by his attendants, parasol, and slave, and his reception by the resident Jesuits. The collection, probably the handsomest ever seen outside Japan, is subsequently to be shown in London, The Hague, and Rome, but, alas, not in America.

The Guggenheim collection of Abstract art from New York shown, appropriately enough, at the *Musée des Arts Decoratifs,* is also being well and seriously received. Presenting the history of Abstract art, it begins in 1895 with a charming Rousseau and a magnificent Cézanne portrait—neither of which could by any stretch of the imagination be called Abstract—goes on through the Cubists, through fine examples of Kandinsky and Chagall, to end with a brilliant and well-chosen display of present-day Action painters, both European and American. The framing of the show is effective and ingenious. A heavy bar of aluminum, an inch deep and a quarter of an inch thick, has been bent to enclose each canvas —an invention at the same time rich, unobtrusive, and becoming to all the pictures.

The great show of seventeenth-century French painting at the *Petit Palais* is little liked. It is claimed that the pictures, principally from provincial museums, were not well selected. At any rate the work displayed seems cold, official and surprisingly Italianate. The oasis in this desert is the group by Georges de la Tour, most of which have not been shown before in Paris—pictures of people by night, illuminated by a single torch or candle. Sometimes the flame is hidden by an arm or hand and one sees the light outlining the sleeve or shining red through the interstices of the fingers—a woman consoling a naked prisoner; St. John dozing, the announcing angel painted as a serious and well-dressed little girl; two women tending by candlelight a swaddled newborn child; a woman in chemise, crushing between her nails a flea. The colors of all the pictures are the same—rich harmonies of pale yellow, black, vermilion, and brown, in complex chiaroscuro. The paint texture has the smooth irregularity of old pottery. The pictures are grave, restrained, and moving, at the same time homely and elegant in a way that is particularly French.

Across the street in the dusty carbarn that is the *Grand Palais,* in its miles and miles of dingy halls, hang the miles and miles of pictures that make up the *Salon des Peintres Independents.* In this exposition without jury one expects to find only two sorts of painters—the amateur or unprofessional, and the young who hope here to be discovered. But there is everything else as well, from the best to the worst, from the most abstruse to the most trite—so much that the eye finds no place to rest and nothing it can remember. One notices only that there is less Abstraction than would be found in a similar American exhibition. The show is impossible to review, impossible even to see. But its very mass demonstrates the devotion of the French to painting and the amazing fertility of the soil from which French painting springs.

In the ground-floor halls, the day I was there, were ranged the thousands of canvases turned down by the jury of the coming *Salon du Printemps.* And as I left I witnessed a touching scene, impossible outside of France—an elderly and beautiful painter, in black, supported by his cane and his tiny wife, and carrying with dignity under his arm a brown paper parcel containing his rejected picture.

## SPRING 1959

The Independents, which each spring precedes the Salon du Printemps in the Paris season, is now at the *Grand Palais*. The *Musée des Arts Decoratifs* is showing a magnificent display of English eighteenth-century furniture, and the seasonal extravagances of the Left Bank include an exhibit of luminous art objects made of blocks of ribbed and spotlighted glass, and a show of Negro-style sculpture crocheted out of starched rope by a real African Negro. The most talked-about shows in town, however, are the French pictures, from Géricault to Matisse, borrowing from Swiss collections; the Toulouse-Lautrecs on loan from Albi; and the exposition of photographs and documents assembled by Sylvia Beach, publisher of *Ulysses*, for the *Centre Culturel Americain*, to commemorate "The Nineteen-twenties; American Writers in Paris and their Friends."

From the point of view of painting, the most important of the three is the show from Switzerland, borrowed from the extraordinary collections of French masters to be found in the small Swiss cities. Baden, for instance, is celebrated for its Cézannes; Winterthur for its Chardins, Van Goghs, and Bonnards; Soleure for its Rouaults and Renoirs. Somewhere in the origin of collections fine as these, a painter is usually to be found. Mary Cassatt, for example, was a friend of the Havermeyers, Duchamp of Arensburg, Glackens of Barnes, Picasso of Gertrude Stein. Thus, it is not surprising to find the traces of a painter here. In 1903, the young Swiss, Charles Montag, had gone to study art in Paris and there discovered Impressionism—a school not yet respectable in Paris, and in Switzerland completely unknown. In his enthusiasm for this new painting, he bought as many pictures as he could afford and obliged his Swiss friends to do likewise. He also invited the painters to Switzerland and introduced them in person to their new collectors. Contrary to what one imagines, these pictures were already no longer cheap. In 1910 Bonnard, at the age of thirty, was already selling for as high as $1,600 and $10,000 had recently been paid for a Cézanne. Montag, however, was well connected and his friends were rich. The result, as can be seen from the present show, was a series of private collections of French nineteenth- and twentieth-century pictures almost without rival.

Seeing these unfamiliar pictures by such well-known painters somewhat revises one's ideas. The Romantic work of Géricault and Delacroix I found one passed by quickly. Corot seems more wonderful than ever, and Monet more important, as does Degas, with a fine red canvas of a woman bathing, and a full-length portrait of Mme. Camus, all in black, at the piano. The Cézanne landscapes, celebrated as they are, seem here less interesting, the colors heavy and clayey. Whereas his portraits are obviously the major pieces of the show—in particular one of the painter himself done in his early forties, wearing a flat black hat and heavy beard, with sunlight falling across the cheekbone; and another of his sister with a fan, seated in a red upholstered chair. Both Bonnard and Vuillard come off well, as does Marquet with his simplified brushwork and beautiful color, and Utrillo's canvas of the Chartres cathedral demonstrates how wonderful a painter he could sometimes, unexpectedly, be. Most curious of all is the importance and stature the great Cubist work of 1911–1913 has now assumed. Twice in my rounds I tried to get near Picasso's *Violon au Café* and Braque's *Jouer de Violon*—both strict Cubist works in brown and tan—and both times the crowd before them was too thick to penetrate.

The Lautrec show at the *Musée Jacquemart-André*—paintings, drawings, lithographs, posters, manuscripts, photographs, and other relics loaned by the Museum of Albi and a few private collectors—has perhaps as its most interesting side the picture it gives of the painter himself. Very few of his large, important paintings are shown. But among the hundred-odd works on view, there is little that is dull and practically nothing one has seen before. It is a very convincing display of the painter's mastery of both the humane and of the decorative styles, his enormous charm as a man. Here are his schoolbooks, scribbled over with drawings and faces, and letters to his mother in schoolboy English. There are photographs of him along with his fellow students in art school, in fancy dress as a Japanese nobleman, and as a choir boy, and even of him swimming in the nude. It is all in the best good humor, as if he were cheerfully accepting his deformity, without self-pity, as a preposterous and entertaining joke. His relation to the café-concert singers and the whore-house personnel who figure so largely in these pictures seems to have been both impersonal and curiously domestic. He saw their character and style, but painted them without glamour, not as a client bedazzled, but with the clear understanding and friendly mockery of a fellow professional. The many small and frequently unfinished works here shown, some of them painted on odd bits of cardboard, are even better evidence than the larger and more famous pieces of the easy accuracy of the painter's eye and of his enormous fecundity. He died too soon; thirty-seven is young for a painter. But then, he had no health. With little expectation of life, he was too hurried. To see it all he had to live too fast. Witness the most pathetic of the objects on display here—his hollow walking cane, made to contain two pints of brandy.

The display at the *Centre Culturel Americain,* which documents the American writers living in Paris in the twenties, is quite disturbing to someone like myself who knew that Paris of between the wars—when living there was cheap and books inexpensive to publish, when the little magazines flourished and American painting students swarmed at Julien's and Colorossi's and all the well-known American composers of today were Nadia Boulanger's students. Here in the array of books, photographs, and manuscripts are all the people one knew or used to see around the Quarter—Hemingway and Bob McAlmon, Gertrude Stein, poet and hostess, mentor and collector of the talented young, Djuna Barnes, Eugene

Jolas, Man Ray, Joyce, Janet Flanner, and Ezra Pound. Here is Sandy Calder (unfortunately without the bent-wire circus he used to animate) and Marcel Duchamp with his enigmatic jokes. Here even is his brown leather valise made to contain, in miniature replica, the complete collection of his works—a portable museum in a traveling salesman's sample case. Here is angel-faced George Antheil, the then wild boy of music, and Aaron Copland who showed up in Paris principally in summer, and Virgil Thomson who lived there, saying that if he had to starve, he preferred to do it where the food was good. It seems unbelievable that this should have already become history and legend. But the show is here to prove it.

## SPRING 1960

Paris in the late spring is flowering with its seasonal exhibitions. The *Salon de Mai*—stylistically the most advanced of the large group shows—is now closed, while the *Salon des Artistes Français* —stylistically the most retrograde—has now opened to display at the *Grand Palais* its miles of unexciting canvases. At the *Musée des Arts Decoratifs,* on the rue de Rivoli side of the Louvre, you can see an impressive array of Louis XIV furniture for five new francs (entrance prices this year are high). And for another five NF the Louvre itself offers the first comprehensive exhibition of Nicholas Poussin ever to be shown—one hundred twenty of his some one hundred eighty known paintings, and one hundred twenty drawings. At the *Petit Palais* is a monster exhibit of art from India —more than a thousand pieces of sculpture and painting ranging over thirty centuries—which the French seem to find laudable but a bit dull. (I, too, would have preferred fewer fragments and more of the pornographic pieces.) Russian officialdom has staged a show of approved painting at the *Musée de l'Art Moderne.* At the *Galerie Charpentier,* Dunoyer de Segonzac, French painter of the prewar School of Paris, is being given, with a too complete retrospective of his fifty years of work, an honorable interment. All this, along with less official shows in private galleries, provides art enough for the most voracious visitor. I found the Poussins and the Russians most provocative.

The Poussin show is enormous—three huge galleries hung with pictures from everywhere—Russia, Spain, even from Australia. The effect is sumptuous. The pictures are rich and somber, as ornate as the Louis XIV style itself of which, in fact, they form a part. One is nevertheless struck by the variations in quality the work displays. On one hand is the wonderful *Inspiration du Poète* belonging to the Louvre, which is as fine as Titian or Veronese, and all the other numerous magnificent examples such as those from the Prado and the Hermitage. On the other hand, there are pictures such as the *Apollon Amoureux de Daphné,* also the Louvre's, which seem quite badly painted. The *Apollo,* Poussin's last work, has most probably been helped to completion by other hands, but the large oval from Copenhagen of *Moses and the Burning Bush* is hard to connect in any way with Poussin. In this anemic work, the flames resemble a modish arrangement of pale blond hair, while one of the two angels supporting the Lord exhibits, somewhat uncanonically, two left feet. But even the undoubtedly authentic works have surprising ups and downs.

This is so in part, I imagine, because in the seventeenth century French painting scarcely yet existed as a school. Poussin was busy inventing it—remodeling the Italian style for home consumption—and was never as much at ease in it as were the Italians themselves. Probably, also, his somewhat provincial public forced him to be more scrupulous and explicit than he would have been for more experienced clients. Hence the painfully exact delineation of features some of these pictures display. Witness for example the *Aenée chez Didon* from the museum at Toledo, Ohio, where all seven faces, including Dido's own reflection in a mirror, are painstakingly and unnecessarily outlined, as if to satisfy the exigence of some provincial buyer. On the other hand, in other works like the Louvre's touching picture of young Adonis dead, the unimportant details of the background figures could not be more skillfully thrown away.

Poussin's way of painting was a somewhat more rigid form of the seventeenth-century Italian technique. As all his drawings prove, he first envisioned his elaborate compositions, with their garlands of figures, as sculpture groups. The pictures were probably first painted, complete in all detail, but only in tones of gray. When this was dry, the carnation of the flesh was put on, and the cold shadows were enlivened with tones of orange and brown. The local colors of the sky, leaves, and costumes were painted in on top of the gray foundation. And the whole was then brushed over with what was termed a "soup"—a transparent glaze of amber pigment thinned in varnish. This amber glaze warmed the cold flesh tones and gave unity to the picture by pulling all the local colors into a single key. One notices how harmoniously cool and dark are the flesh tones in those pictures which—like those of the Louvre or Prado—have not suffered undue restoration. In certain of the others, however, the final glazes have apparently been lost in excessive cleaning, for the bodies have a glassy emphasis, and the blue of the sky and draperies a vitreous brilliance, which were certainly not in the original intention.

I find it easier to esteem than love these complex arabesques of figures in pagan and Biblical settings. Admirable as they are in skill of hand and composition, their somewhat official coldness seems to anounce the even more frigid historical set-pieces of David and Ingres. On the other hand, those of the paintings which are really landscapes, but drawn into the noble style by the arbitrary imposition of some small classical reference, excite all my admiration. There is one from Dulwich College: I have forgotten the classical subject and remember only a tranquil, shaded road near Rome. In such as these Poussin invented the type itself of serene landscape which all subsequent French painting has so beautifully exploited.

The Russian and Soviet painting show is of another order. Let me begin by saying that among the one hundred sixty-four works exhibited, there are two quite good pictures. One is a small nineteenth-century oil by Alexis Venetsianov, charming in drawing and color—a pleasantly realistic representation of a peasant asleep on the ground in a flat farm country. The other is a pale and delicate landscape of birches and thawing river in early spring, done in 1945 by Serge Guerassimov. Along with these there are some undistinguished eighteenth- and nineteenth-century pictures. The rest of the show seems to be made up of all the most showy and shoddy work that could be found in a French salon of the epoch of 1909.

Here indeed is painting addressed to a provincial public. Each picture tells a story. Most are garish in color; all are insistently labored and detailed. The more advanced of the painters advertise their modernism by some flashy mannerism of brushwork or drawing. The more imposing depict in brutal chiaroscuro some touching domestic scene or lurid anecdote. There is, for example, Yablonskaia's *Le Matin,* a large brash picture of a young girl just out of bed and beginning her ballet exercises; and Ioganson's huge picture of a former rich mineowner and his former poor employees glaring at one another with contempt and hatred; and The Koukrynisky's larger and even more theatrical *"Kaput,"* showing the end of Hitler and his staff in the cellars of the Reich. (The Koukrynisky is the trade name for three different painters who work and sign together as a firm, doubtless to demonstrate that painting need not be an individualistic art.) Tasteless, vulgar, and commercial, these works have little in common with any serious tradition of painting. In kind and quality they resemble rather the illustrations to popular novels of before the First World War. But even in technical dexterity and the skill of storytelling, none of them is nearly as good as our own Norman Rockwell.

Let us hope that the selections were badly made. Certainly, the pre-Soviet pictures seem to have been chosen with little acumen. Somewhere in Russia there must be better painting. One must remember that this is an official selection, made on doctrinal and extra-professional principles, of the same order as that which last year moved us to send an exhibit of Abstract Expressionists to represent all of our own country's painting at the Brussels Fair.

I am nevertheless extremely glad I went. The *Musée de l'Art Moderne* contains in permanent display the finest and most complete array of School of Paris pictures it is possible to see—Bonnard, Vuillard, Marquet, Picasso and all the rest, along with unexpectedly fine paintings by less-known names, as well as a delightful room of the contemporary primitives; all this without any of the educational insistence and Germanizing tendency which give our own New York Museum of Modern Art its somewhat oppressive tone.

## FALL 1961

The particularly wet Paris winter—it has been raining steadily since the 14th of July—is also distinguished by some extraordinary exhibitions. The *Petit Palais*, with the help of the Italian Government, is showing a splendid array of the eighteenth-century Italian painters. The Louvre has opened its new top-floor galleries with some seven hundred pictures drawn from its reserves—pictures which changes in taste or lack of wall space had hitherto consigned to the cellars. Most exciting of all, the show that has all Paris talking hangs at the *Musée de l'Art Moderne*—paintings, posters, architecture, furniture, and decoration done between 1884 and 1914, and chosen to illustrate "The Sources of the Twentieth Century."

The Italian show somewhat surprises the French, who are apt to think that they own the eighteenth century. The great novelty here is the genre painting of the Neopolitan Gaspare Traversi, beautifully executed, full of good humor, caricature, and tenderness. I particularly remember a picture of a not very seriously *Wounded Man*, just in from a street brawl, his scratches being treated by a pretentious doctor and a very pretty maid. There is a room of Piranesi's *Ruins* and *Prisons*, a number of Pannini's highly detailed views of court ceremonies in Rome, and fine Magnascos of monks leading their insectlike communal life. The Venetians make up more than half the show. There are the best Piazettas I have seen, of pretty ladies with their parasols and lovely clothes and doll-like faces; a complete display of the landscapes of Canaletto, Belotto and Guardi; and wonderful Tiepolos, both father and son.

The Louvre's exhibit falls sharply into two sections—old masters and the nineteenth century. The galleries of the older paintings are crowded and difficult to inspect—too many pictures on too many tiers. Despite the presence of many fine things, the general effect is of an exposition at a public auction hall. The nineteenth-century galleries, on the other hand, are a delight, with all sorts of things one remembers with affection from the Louvre of other times. There are wonderful portraits by David; *La Source* of Ingres, so sweet and shy and plump, and his *Oedipus and the Sphinx* where Oedipus with jaw-line beard and delicately muscled feet resembles a Beaux Arts student consulting his professor. There is the well-remembered portrait of two sisters by Chassériau and Whistler's mother looking very content to be home again in the mild Paris damp. There are any number of Delacroix and almost fifty Corots of all periods, even including his wall decorations for a bathroom. The Daubigny landscapes stand up beautifully. The Rousseaus and Diazes now seem less good. There are beautiful small Millets along with those two popular favorites *The Gleaners* and *The Angelus*, which both turn out to be as awful as one remembers. There is even a small collection of Impressionists. It is all very pleasant and instructive.

Considerably more impressive is "The Sources of the Twentieth Century" at the *Musée de l'Art Moderne*. This show is without doubt the best thing of the sort ever done. It is enormous—like a world's fair exhibit—and covers the whole field of advanced art from the middle of the eighties to the beginning of the First World War. The period is defined as one goes in (through a Paris Metro station entrance by Hector Guimard in the Art Nouveau style) by a mural-size photograph of the Eiffel Tower still in construction. The displays of architecture and decoration are particularly successful and complete, with examples of furniture and models and photographs of buildings by everybody from the Scotch Mackintosh to the Catalan Gaudi. It is the first time I have seen the Art Nouveau exhibited without comic effect. The German furniture on display, one cannot deny, is hideously ugly. But the French versions, by Gallé, Majorelle, Guimard, and the others, prove to be rich, solid, comfortable, of a workmanship unknown today, and not in any way funny.

The most impressive part of the show, however, is the painting. It is all there—from the Impressionism of Monet and Degas to the beginnings of Dada in Duchamp and Picabia—and not only from the School of Paris, which one expects, but from all the rest of Europe as well: the Italian Pointillists and Futurists; the Nordic followers of Gauguin and of the Symbolists (the inept Willumsen with his hand-carved frames, and Ensor and Munch and August Strindberg, better known as dramatist than as painter); and two rooms of German Expressionists, the finest I have ever seen. Along with this goes a sumptuous display of commercial and theatrical posters by everybody from Mucha and Cheret to Lautrec and Villon.

Looked at in detail, the painting offers frequent surprises. The greatest, perhaps, is how badly the Cézannes show up. Perhaps the white walls of the museum, so flattering to decorative painting, are too harsh for Cézanne's dark tonalities. The *Cirque* by Seurat is even more dead in color—perhaps it has now faded—and its execution seems both tedious and amateurish.

On the other hand, the painting of Van Gogh and of Odilon Redon—usually not my particular favorites—shine out like jewels, second only to the extraordinary display of Gauguins. Gauguin's companions, Sérusier and Emile Bernard, whom I have not hitherto seen, are also there. Bernard, so much a figure in the Van Gogh and Gauguin letters, turns out to be quite bad, as does the once-celebrated mural painter, Puvis de Chavannes. The display of Fauves is splendid and complete, my favorite being a reclining nude by Van Dongen, and there is a spectacular room of Bonnard, Vuillard, and the other *Nabis*. There are early blue pictures of Picasso and by his

Catalan friend, Nonell y Monturiol, who died at twenty-nine; early and surprisingly unmannered Modiglianis; all the Cubists, including an astonishing Léger with pieces of looking glass set in; all the Italian Futurists with their breath-taking complexity; the Duchamp *Nude* and the Mondrian *Tree;* along with the Douanier Rousseau's big *Serpent Charmer* which, to my great surprise, seems in no way out of place among all these Cubists, and not even naïve.

Nevertheless, from all this vigor and variety and fecundity one carries away some very curious impressions: first, of a movement uniquely devoted to the pursuit of novelty and the exploitation of mannerism. The second impression is even more disturbing. Is it possible that Modern art came to an end with the beginning of the First World War? Certainly little new has since been added to the work shown here. Surrealism and Neo-Romanticism, which came after the war, were extensions of subject matter rather than advances in technique. And the ideas and practices which serve our Abstract Expressionism were already present in the sources of Dada.

At any rate the modern school in France seems sad enough today, if one is to believe the Galerie Charpentier's show entitled "School of Paris 1960." This, though it was selected by a group of best-known critics, might be a sampling from any current official salon. There are a few crude or mannered representational works, some rather more skillful Crypto-Impressionist paintings (the subject of the picture half-readable through an abstract overlay), along with a great many pure Abstractions in the various known modes—the most original being an unsigned flesh-pink canvas slashed with five vertical strokes of a razor blade.

Titillatingly cruel as this may be, it seems scarcely worth the five new francs it costs to see it. I think I would like better the "contactual nudes," shown last summer at the Galerie Rive Droite. These I am very sorry to have missed; for, as I was later told by friends in Paris, the painter, Yves Klein, created them before a select audience at his vernissage by dipping live models in paint and rolling them on canvas.

# *Victor Hugo*

THE PLACE DES VOSGES, with its uniform façades of pink brick and warm gray stone, is one of the noblest examples in Paris of seventeenth-century architectural design. No. 6, where Victor Hugo lived—a corner house overlooking both the square and the playground of the school next door—is maintained as a museum to house the great man's personal mementos and literary relics. All four floors of the building are decorated after the taste of his times in dark red damask and dark varnished wood. The occasion for my visit was the small additional exhibit now being held to commemorate the centenary of *La Légende des Siècles,* an epic poem judged by many to be the finest in French since the *Chanson de Roland.*

French admiration for Hugo is grudging but sincere. Remember Cocteau's celebrated little joke that Victor Hugo was a madman who believed he was Victor Hugo; and Gide, when asked who was the greatest French poet, said, "Victor Hugo, alas!" All this one knows. What one is less likely to know is that Hugo was also an admirable painter. To prove it, there hang in his museum—alongside the family portraits and all the insipid illustrations to his writings by contemporary artists—some three hundred fifty drawings and water colors by Hugo himself. Their freedom and vigor are incomparably more impressive than the Victorian niceties of the professional work on show beside them.

These pictures range from tiny album-leaf sketches to water colors almost four feet long. The colors are restrained and somber

—blacks, grays, browns, and tans—done in pen, brush, India ink, and sepia. The lighting is dramatic: the tamest of the architectural drawings has a nightmare quality. The boldness of the brushwork and the systematic use of spattering, smearing, and scratching to vary tone and texture make the pictures strangely like the drawings of Bérard, Tchelitchew, Brien Gysin, and the other neo-Romantic painters of our time. Which is not surprising, since Hugo was a real Romantic.

The subjects are elaborate and varied; travel sketches from France, England, along the Rhine, imaginary landscapes; illustrations for his books; a castle in Spain; the cathedral at Rheims, crouching on its low hill like a hurt animal; the hand of an abbess raised in benediction; a nude in bed; an abandoned cannon; a fisherwoman watching the sea in storm; fanciful variations on his own initials; the sewers of Paris seen from within and portrayed as the bowels of a leviathan; fantastic animals; horrid or malicious caricatures such as *Mlle. George in Amorous Undress,* wherein the celebrated actress is shown standing, a vacuous mountain of flesh, naked in an open robe de chambre; *The Eddystone Lighthouse,* flying the Union Jack and laced with mottos, as jerry-built and rickety and improvised as if to represent the British Empire itself.

Painting skill of this order is surprising in a writer. A great many painters write, some extremely well. The list is unending—from Vasari and Michelangelo to Van Gogh and Dali. But the writers whose paintings can be taken seriously are very few. With the possible exception of Leonardo (who, I believe, thought of himself as man of science first and painter afterwards), William Blake is the only other besides Hugo I can recall offhand. And just as the painter-writers for the most part write about painting, it is not surprising that Blake and Hugo, the writer-painters, both paint about writing. That is to say, their pictures announce moods, or illustrate ideas, more fully developed elsewhere in their literary work. And, satisfied with the immediate effectiveness of water color, neither

Blake nor Hugo had any need to attempt the more difficult problems of painting in oil.

But here the likeness ends. Blake lived in England where the tradition of painting was insular and new: the English School was begun by Hogarth only sixty years before him. Blake, besides, was a medievalist in revolt against his century and his century's ways. The manner of painting he devised for himself was a form of pre-Rubensism, more limited and insular even than the tradition he refused to follow. Consequently, his pictures, however interesting to the literary world, are too affected and provincial to have any place in the history of painting. Hugo, on the other hand, had no such reserves about his times. Living in a period of intense artistic activity, in constant contact with painting and painters, he was able to turn out pictures whose force, invention and originality are still impressive today.

Not satisfied with being a painter, Hugo was a decorator as well. What a delightful dining room he designed and executed for Juliette Drouet, his mistress! Its style is a sort of nineteenth-century Chinese-Rococo with racks and cabinets and ornate fireplace made to frame a collection of Chinese plates and porcelain figurines. The panels are incised in pyrography with dragons and tiny comic Chinese personages, and painted black and gold and green and red in imitation lacquer—handsome and extraordinarily professional. Of the personal souvenirs the most touching to me is a mirror, adorned by Hugo with birds and flowers, which carries this dedication to his young son:

> Passereaux et rouges-gorges
> Venez des airs et des eaux,
> Venez tous faire vos orges,
> Messieurs les petits oiseaux,
> Chez Monsieur le petit Georges.

One is reminded, after all, that Hugo was a poet.

# *L'envoi*

THERE ARE a great many pictures in the world, and a great many people find great pleasure in looking at them. Many of us, on the other hand, get no pleasure from them at all. The principal purpose of painting, I am sure, is to give pleasure; and if these pictures, despite their accepted excellence, fail to give it, something must be wrong with our way of looking at them. Perhaps we are asking too much—looking for the wrong things in them or expecting emotions the art of painting is not designed to provide. Is there not some sure and dependable method of receiving from art the pleasures it was unquestionably intended to give?

We have all heard how a party of Japanese tourists will climb a mountain and all together, without the slightest loss of dignity, bend double to contemplate the landscape through their divided legs. What this artistically sophisticated race is accustomed to do in front of nature, we should certainly find advantageous to practice in front of art. Let us then assume this Japanese posture, and standing with our backs toward a picture, bend forward and examine it through the space between our knees. This, at first sight, may appear an irreverent attitude to take before a work of art. But, though it imposes the bodily glow of a setting-up exercise upon the more spiritual delights of artistic appreciation, it is not as impertinent as it seems. It serves a very practical purpose.

The work of art in front of which our observer is reversing himself has two quite different aspects—as subject matter and as composition. The subject matter depends a great deal for its readability on the laws of gravity. Viewed upside down, it is greatly incommoded. Unable to communicate reasonably with the spectator, it tends to efface itself and becomes illegible. Not so for the composition. In a well-composed picture the lines of construction are comfortable in any position. Consequently, by reversing himself before a work of art, the observer is enabled to disregard its subject matter—nowadays a persistent source of confusion in any artistic evaluation—and can judge the painting by the much more familiar criteria of Abstract design.

Nevertheless, I am afraid that the Japanese position may prove ill-suited to public performance. Present-day tailoring renders the attitude difficult. Turning the picture upside down is no easier solution. In a private house, nothing is more difficult than rehanging pictures. And in a museum the guards are there to oppose any attempt at rearrangement. Let us examine another perhaps more satisfactory solution. Let us try to look at a picture as the painter does.

The painter looks at a picture around his thumb, or across his brush, or framed by his two hands, or through a window formed by his thumb and forefinger. Can this method be recommended to the aspiring art appreciator without reserve?

I am afraid it cannot. The painter's sighting tricks are a device not of appreciation but of analysis—for discovering if something in a picture is out of key or out of measure. With his thumb held up he blocks out a troublesome spot and can see how the picture would look without it. Holding his brush horizontal or vertical at arm's length, he measures distances and compares sizes. With the shadow box made by his hands he limits and frames a motif in nature to see how it would look transported to his canvas. Looking through the little window of his thumb and forefinger he isolates a particular passage in his subject or in his painting and examines it alone, uninfluenced by neighboring lines or shapes or values or colors. He is not making an esthetic judgment; he is studying visual detail. The gestures by which he does this are professional ones. For a layman to use them would be pretentious. To employ them becomingly our layman must go through a certain amount of training: several years of art school, a course in life drawing, considerable working with colors, canvases, and brushes, a certain amount of copying pictures in museums, finishing off with perhaps a short stay in Provincetown. And in the end all his efforts may miscarry. Instead of simply having learned to use without embarrassment the painter's gestures, the aspirant is likely to find that he has overshot his mark and become a painter himself.

Let us by all means keep him a layman. As a layman he has still another approach to the gustation of pictures, the one offered by our institutions of higher learning. In every college and university there is a department devoted to the appreciation of art through the study of its history. Here the aspirant can learn to look at pictures, not in the awkward posture of the Japanese nor yet with the esoteric gestures of the painter, but in the sober and reputable attitude of the scholar. He will learn the dates of pictures, their schools, manners, derivations, iconologies, and problematical attributions; also the lives of their painters, the history of the guilds, the history of criticism, the technique of the authentication of masterpieces by the correlation of documents, in fact the complete story of painters, painting, and collecting. If he takes all the courses he will have learned everything that is currently taught about pictures—everything except how to find in one of them pleasure or companionship.

So far all we have are ways of looking at pictures for information; no enjoyment or intimacy is involved at all. To add to our discomfort, a picture is a piece of property that in most cases belongs to someone else—a painter or a rich man or a dealer or a museum—and consequently can be inspected only under fairly trying circumstances. In the museum we are surrounded by guards, crowds, marble halls, acres of art, too many things to look at, too many people. At the picture dealer's the danger of buying lurks about us and we sense how easily we can be compromised by an admiring word. In the home of the collector we are congealed in the deep freeze of a luxury not our own. And in the painter's studio we are terrified of saying the wrong thing, or the right thing about the wrong picture.

Even greater than the terror of saying the wrong thing is that of feeling the wrong thing. We have all heard about something called the esthetic emotion. But here we stand in front of our picture and we feel no emotion at all. A sense of personal inadequacy overwhelms us and we are with difficulty restrained from rushing out of the museum or the gallery or the collection or the studio to the waiting room of the nearest psychiatrist. For something, we are sure, must be wrong.

Indeed, something is wrong, but not with us. What is wrong is our constant expectation of emotion. A composer of music deals with emotion. He can describe an emotional state so accurately that the listener can recognize it and re-experience it. But a painter's technique was never made for massaging the solar plexus. It is all for holding the eye. The painter renders a visual idea, something he has seen, if only in his mind's eye. If the resulting picture is successful, it in turn will be interesting to look at and can be remembered by the eye.

Anyway, all easy emotion is suspect. In this age of commercialized propaganda and mass appeal, the rarest and most precious thing we can experience is simple communication, as from man to man. The test of whether a picture is any good—that is to say any good for you, which is the only thing that counts—is not whether it thrills you but whether you can remember it. If you walk casually and rapidly through a picture gallery, just as you would walk through a friendly crowd, and on leaving find that you can remember some visual detail from one of the pictures—a face, a gesture, a line, a color, anything at all—it means that there has been communication between you and that picture and that that particular picture is probably worth going back to look at again. Do not bother yourself about good or bad taste. Look for communication. If you remember something from the Landseer you have just seen and nothing from the Picasso, leave the Picasso be and go back one day for another look at the Landseer. Of if you remember something from Picasso, do not be afraid of following a too-current fashion; go back for another look at the Picasso. The more clearly you remember any picture, the more complete has been the communication.

When I speak of remembering the picture, I do not mean remembering its subject matter—its anecdotal, poetic, or Freudian references—but remembering the picture itself as something seen—as lines, shapes, colors, forms, gestures, faces, things that cannot be described satisfactorily in words but can only fully exist as images for the eye. However useful the subject matter may have been to the painter in inspiring him to complete or enabling him to sell his picture, the humanistic value lies not in its verbal associations, in its Freudian or any other kind of devotional orthodoxy, but in its ability to communicate to the spectator something the painter has once seen and make him remember it.

Nevertheless, a picture is not a simple view. It is a view that has been passed through a painter's mind. It has gone in at his eye and come out at his hand. In that passage it has become opaque, personal, dubious, devious, and obscure. For it has become the painter himself—not the painter being sociable at a party but the man alone, face to face with his subject, his materials, and his vocation. And even though at first sight the picture may appear transparent, frank, and clear, this openness is misleading. It is only a surfacing, an outer layer thin as an onion skin. Beneath it the picture is as mysterious as any other living thing; even more, because it is the concentration of a living essence. It is secure, self-possessed, and arrogant.

Consequently you cannot force yourself upon a picture any more than you can force yourself upon a prince. It will not give itself that way. Besides, we are not simple autograph collectors; we want friends, not a list of names. Treat the picture like a celebrity and it will snub you. Like a celebrity it will show you only its mask. Sitting down in front of it and saying "now tell me all about yourself" will not do, either. The picture can no more respond to such a demand than could the painter or anyone else. Valid human communication takes tact and an open mind, warmth, self-respect. A picture is a personage and must be approached as one.

And here at last is the true and proper way to look at a picture. Let us call it "inspection by indirection." Suppose the presentation has been made; you have passed by a picture and something from it sticks in your mind. The next step is to allow the picture to become accustomed to you. This means at least several visits. Let us hope, for your convenience, that it hangs in a private house where you are in the habit of going and where you feel at home. But a museum will do if it is a comfortable museum where you are not pushed around by guards or bustled by crowds or awed by authorities. Now comes the most important thing: do not look at the picture. Let the picture look at you. You must ignore it politely. If you glance at it at all, it must be out of the corner of the eye in passing. Exert no undue effort to make the picture's acquaintance. Do not be eager or inviting. If the picture finds you interesting, intelligent, sympathetic, in any other way worthy of its advances, it will force itself on your attention, become part of your private life, and claim a friend's prerogatives to change your way of looking at the world. And you may justifiably boast "I like that picture, and I suspect as well it also likes me."

# INDEX